Kia hiwa ra! Listen to culture
—Māori students' plea to educators

Angus H Macfarlane

NEW ZEALAND COUNCIL FOR EDUCATIONAL RESEARCH

TE RŪNANGA O AOTEAROA MŌ TE RANGAHAU I TE MĀTAURANGA

Wellington 2004

New Zealand Council for Educational Research
PO Box 3237
Wellington
New Zealand

ISBN 1-877293-29-6

Cover photograph by courtesy of Ngongotahā School

Printed by PrintLink
Wellington

Distributed by NZCER Distribution Services
PO Box 3237
Wellington
New Zealand
www.nzcer.org.nz

Contents

ACKNOWLEDGMENTS

Ko te whakaariki, ko te whakaariki,

Tukua mai ki a piri, tukua mai ki a tata, kia eke mai,

Ki runga ki te paepae poto a Houmaitawhiti e

Ka mihi, ka tangi, ka aroha ra ki o tātou tini mate e hinga ana i runga i o tatou marae o te motu. Ka huri ki a tātou ngā morehu a aitua – kei te mihi, kei te mihi. Ka huri hoki ki te kaupapa, arā, ngā mahi o nga kaiako whakaharahara hei tauira mo tatou.

The writing of this book was made possible through my being awarded a Senior Research Fellowship by the New Zealand Council for Educational Research in Wellington. To Robyn Baker and the staff at NZCER, thank you for the faith you had in me and for your professional support during the semester I had with you in 2003. Several organisations and their characters feature in this book and deserve a special mention. These include Ngongotahā School and Terry Morrison, Gaye Ruru, and Bev Anaru. In addition, I acknowledge Tangaroa College and Mike Leach and David Riley. I also pay tribute to the contributions that Sonja Bateman made as she recounted, in Chapter Eight, some of her classroom experiences. This project was mentored by Bev Webber, processed to print by Carlene Grigg, and edited by Anne Else . . . I thank you sincerely.

Heoi anō ko te tūmanako, ma te Runga Rawa koutou, otirā tātou katoa, hei manaaki, hei tiaki i ngā wā katoa.

Angus H Macfarlane

PREFACE

A key theme underlying this book is the role that culture plays in education and the implications of that role for teaching and teachers, and for learning and learners. Culture is what has been learned from experiences in the environment and is reflected in the ways that people interact with their environment. Sensitivity to the cultural background of Māori students is seen as especially important for educators, because educators who are culturally sensitive will be more able to understand, and respond to the learning needs of today's diverse classrooms. While the content of this book orients toward working with Māori students, many of the ideas and strategies can be introduced and implemented for all students who make up these diverse classrooms.

The content of the book is largely drawn from research I carried out for my doctoral studies in 2000 and 2001. At that time I investigated three contrasting educational sites within my iwi of Te Arawa, each of which were known to be effective in making a difference for Māori students. One of those sites, the Ngāti-Whakaue Enrichment Class at Ngongotahā School is referred to in this book, although culturally responsive pedagogy was a feature of all three sites.

Chapter One sets the scene by tracing the frustrations of Māori education in the past, but it does not dwell there. Despite the disturbing patterns in Māori academic underachievement that have been and continue to be seen in educational reports and the media, models of successful practices do exist, and these provide hope. Chapter Two proposes that hope can be converted to reality if people were to "listen to culture". Chapters Three through to Six describe the pedagogical underpinnings of the Ngāti-Whakaue Enrichment Class. While this is a small sample (twelve children), enough evidence was gathered from a national award-winning teacher and her ecological context to suggest that the educational needs of Māori students were being successfully addressed. From this, Chapter Seven offers messages for teachers. An important message outlined in this chapter is that while classroom teachers need to find generic teaching strategies that work for all students, these strategies should be culturally appropriate and persistent in terms of representing and affirming the culture and language of Māori students.

Chapter Eight offers strategies for teachers in diverse classrooms. It is not easy to come up with "purely" Māori teaching strategies. There are, however, Māori-preferred learning and teaching strategies. What guided me in this chapter was the wisdom of a kuia of Ngāti Ranginui and Ngai te Rangi, Rangiwhakaehu Walker, affectionately known as Aunty Nan. In 2001 I took my postgraduate class to Group Special Education's Poutama Pounamu Education Research and Development Centre at Tauranga. In the course of some discussion, one of my students asked Aunty Nan about the "specific" strategies that work well for Māori students experiencing learning and behaviour difficulties. Aunty Nan referred to "whakawhanaungatanga" (building relationships) as a key strategy, from which other techniques evolve. The response from the kuia was superb. She saw the big picture from within a Māori frame of reference, a framework that had the capability to guide professional knowledge and intercultural communication. I attribute the core principles that underpin the content of this chapter to Aunty Nan's insightfulness. In this chapter, five Māori frames of reference (whanaungatanga, rangatiratanga, manaakitanga, kotahitanga, and pumanawatanga) extend to teachers an "educultural" approach to classroom management. Classroom practice is perceived as so complex, yet its success stories (as in this chapter) can be stated in two words: the teachers.

The final chapter reiterates the argument that a central characteristic of programmes that attend successfully to Māori students' achievement is cultural centredness.

CHAPTER ONE

Educational provision for Māori: fortitude in the face of frustration

Recent developments in the New Zealand political landscape, the economic uncertainty of the times, the rapidly-changing demographic characteristics of the school-aged populations, and the concern expressed about many social problems affecting young people have reignited the arguments over the roles schools are expected to play in preparing children and adolescents for productive futures (Brown and Simons, 1997). In addition, the changing demographic characteristics of New Zealand schools reflect global trends, where the number and diversity of minority students attending schools is on the increase.

Throughout the last three decades, concern has been frequently expressed about the lower achievement and higher suspension rates of Māori students, compared with their non-Māori counterparts. In 1973 the Minister of Education, Phil Amos, commissioned a review to study the problems arising from suspensions in secondary schools, and the growing concern over the problem of effective communication between schools and parents (Department of Education, 1973). This review identified issues relating to a range of programmes, including teacher training and pastoral care for Māori students at risk of failure. The report made 65 recommendations to the Minister with, it would seem, accuracy and integrity. Since that time, students have been presenting schools with increasingly severe and diverse learning and behaviour problems. Māori children continue to be over-represented at the negative end of the continuum.

By the end of the 1990s, on average, 68 students were being suspended every day from New Zealand schools. Officially, a total of 6,145 students were suspended in the first half of 1997 (Ministry of Education figures, quoted in New Zealand Education Review, 16 September 1997). This was more than double the number of suspensions in 1992. What was once largely a secondary school phenomenon is now happening much more frequently in primary schools too. Suspensions by primary schools have shown a dramatic increase over the last few years. Concerns over the growing number of Māori students being suspended from school were raised at a parliamentary select committee in September, 1998. The committee was told that 40 percent, or two out of every five, of the students suspended from school between 1992 and 1996 were Māori. Yet Māori made up only 20 percent of students (New Zealand Education Review, 1997). Since 1992, the number of Māori students suspended had increased by 132 percent, nearly twice the rate of increase for non-Māori (at 73 percent). In Hamilton schools, during 1996, 219 Māori students were suspended from their schools, compared with 158 non-Māori students (Ministry of Education, Suspension Statistics Report, 1996). This trend was also evident in the statistics from other areas of New Zealand. More recent statistics (Ministry of Education, 2002) show that while moderate improvements have been made in reducing the suspension rates of Māori students, the discrepancy for them compared with other ethnic groups, continues to raise concerns. A range of New Zealand research on children who experience behavioural and emotional difficulties reports that the ethnic group most often represented is Māori (Burgess, 1992; Clark, Smith, and Pomare, 1996; Report of the Education and Science Committee, 1995; Galloway, 1985; Kelly, 1990; Macfarlane, 1995). Many of these Māori students seem to become alienated within mainstream schooling, and are often excluded from it.

Many explanations have been suggested for why a higher percentage of Māori students are expelled from the success routes at school, and are more frequently represented in alternative education programmes, or end up on the streets. Thirty years ago, Ranginui Walker (1973) identified issues that continue to be major problems for New Zealand education. The first is that most teachers in New Zealand schools are non-Māori and monocultural. He contends that many lack the skills, knowledge, and sensitivity to be able to teach effectively in a multi-ethnic classroom. Walker refers to a Pākehā frame of reference, which often stereotypes Māori success as restricted to limited domains such as sport and music. Add to this the notion that conventional schools appear to run counter to important Māori cultural values, and the issue of incompatibility of cultures presents a major challenge.

Bishop (1996), and Bishop and Glynn (1999) add to this argument the issue of power imbalance. They assert that the denial of the importance of cultural identity is a key feature of power imbalances in New Zealand education. Bishop and Glynn (1999, p. 131) refer to "a pattern of dominance and subordination and its constituent classroom interaction patterns (pedagogy) that perpetuates the non-participation of many young Māori people in the benefits that the education system has to offer". They identify teachers as retaining power over issues of initiation, benefits, representation, legitimation, and accountability, mainly by creating and participating in teaching contexts that represent the knowledge bases, beliefs, values, and practices of a western worldview. Further, Booth and Coulby (cited in Garner and Gains, 1996) claim that most teachers who have dealt with problematic student behaviour would probably agree that it is usually accompanied by underachievement in the formal curriculum. They go on to claim that much of the student behaviour regarded as disruptive is a consequence of inappropriate curricula.

Others argue that the reason for the disadvantage and underachievement of Māori students lies in the socio-economic differences between Māori and non-Māori, rather than in the cultural mismatch between western schooling and Māori cultural values (Fergusson, Horwood, and Lloyd, 1991; Harker and Nash, 1996). Harker (1978) suggests that both socio-economic and cultural factors are central in accounting for variance in school achievement. He refers first to the environmental deprivation model, which explains Māori underachievement in terms of low occupational status, large families, and rural residence; and secondly to the cultural difference model. Walker (1973) summarises the cultural difference model as predominantly monocultural, perpetuating a western middle class orientation, which is often irrelevant to Māori and has the potential to alienate students. The cultural difference model asserts that educational achievement for minority culture students reflects the social and cultural influences of the school environment (Steele, cited in Brown and Simons, 1997). This view reflects a more transactional perspective, where environments and individuals interact with and select each other to produce a given outcome.

In a third model, an interaction model of educational achievement also proposed by Steele, two kinds of outcome seem possible. The first type of outcome draws on Steele's (1992) study in the mid-Atlantic region. This study attributed differing African-American achievement to the stigma these students endure in the educational environment. This stigma arises both from teachers and from peers who assume their intellectual inferiority, as well as from the constant demands they face to "prove themselves" at every level of schooling. Ogbu (1983) suggests that one possible reason for many minority students failing at school is to do with attitudes of either the student or his or her peers, which see doing well in school as at odds with their ethnic group's educational status. Ritchie (1963) discusses the whakamā (shyness) concept in terms of individual Māori identity. In that context, institutions such as family and school have been known to apply sanctions which play no small role in shaping the behaviour of Māori children. Often frustrated, the child says, in effect, "I am Māori, Māori is bad, I am bad; and the Pākehā (European) world confirms this judgement later on" (Ritchie, 1963, p. 183).

These trains of thought imply that coming from a minority or indigenous culture into a mainstream school constitutes a deficit in terms of school expectations, and that there is a deficit association between ethnicity, academic performance, and behavioural responses. This reinforces the central role of schools in explaining or accounting for the underachievement of Māori students, who may be judged at risk because of their ethnicity. Hamilton (1992) argues that many Māori children have a different outlook on life from the non-Māori children around them. Many teachers and schools ignore this, either intentionally or unintentionally, by asserting they are "treating all children the same" (Hamilton, p. 55). When the powerful dominant culture asserts that all children are the same, there is a real danger that individual differences, cultural identities, and culturally preferred values and practices will be marginalised or ignored. This has been the outcome for many Māori over more than a century of state education in New Zealand.

The second type of outcome is more positive, because some researchers have found a positive relationship between ethnic identity and school achievement. For example, Bowman and Howard's study (cited in Brown and Simons, 1997) of African-American youths found that students whose parents had proactively given them strategies to deal with educational barriers achieved higher grades. They postulated that these strategies also improved the students' sense of personal efficacy. In New Zealand, this type of outcome appears to be more evident, particularly in educational environments where power imbalances are being addressed. Graham Smith (1992) contends that during the last two decades, Māori people have become more assertive and more self-interested in protecting and promoting their language and culture. It is urgent, according to Smith, to repair the schooling and education enterprise so that it can deliver fairly and justly for Māori.

The Te Kōhanga Reo (Language Nest) movement, which began in 1982, has been an exciting development in Māori education. This offers an all-Māori language and culture immersion environment for children from birth to school age. The aim is to develop children within a context replicating a Māori home where only Māori language is spoken and heard. The kōhanga reo are open to all children of all cultures, and have proved to be very popular (Irwin and Davies, cited in McInerney and McInerney, 1998). Following on from this is the increasing provision of bilingual and bicultural education from primary school (kura kaupapa), through to secondary school (wharekura). The first official kura kaupapa Māori was established in 1985 at Hoani Waititi Marae in Auckland. Vercoe (1999) observes that like its predecessor, Te Kōhanga Reo, Kura Kaupapa Māori was initiated outside state control, and without state funding. Its existence was maintained by a determined community effort to address the lack of educational programmes and equality of outcomes for Māori children. According to Kuni Jenkins and Ka'ai (cited in Coxon, Jenkins, Marshall, and Massey, 1994), kura kaupapa's resistance to state-driven imperatives placed it at the leading edge of the Māori renaissance, and firmly established it as the spearhead for Māori initiatives into the new century.

The importance of kura kaupapa Māori lies in their attempt to situate learning in the appropriate cultural context. Corson (1993, p. 56) says that these schools:

> . . . try to restore mana (status, prestige) of the Māori learner in a meaningful way by creating an environment where Māori culture is the taken-for-granted background against which everything else is set. For the pupils, being Māori in Te Kura Kaupapa is the norm; the school and classroom environment connects with the Māori home; cultural and language values are central; Māori parents make decisions for their children unimpeded by majority culture gatekeeping devices; and the whānau (extended family group) assumes responsibility for the education of their children along with control and direction of the school itself. At the same time, these schools are concerned to teach a modern, up-to-date and relevant curriculum, following national guidelines set by the state, whose outcome will be the production of bilingual and bicultural graduates.

Vercoe (1999) adds that kura kaupapa philosophies embrace the concepts, practices, and beliefs of Te Ao Māori (the Māori world) mainly by propounding a specific commitment to the survival of Māori knowledge. Fearing that these elements would be bastardised through institutionalism, the philosophy known as Te Aho Mātua (traditions of the ancestors) was conceived and became the cultural agenda by which a school was given a mandate to become kura kaupapa Māori. It is this aspect that distinguishes kura kaupapa from other Māori language programmes, such as Total Immersion Units and Bilingual Units. There is no question that te kōhanga reo and kura kaupapa Māori have gained the support of many Māori parents. The children who attend these schools may have less chance of experiencing a crisis of cultural identity, compared with their counterparts in mainstream schools. This assumption is largely premised on the fact that they are taught within a context that is culturally Māori. It should also be acknowledged that in mainstream schools, there are numerous accounts of Māori students whose successes are an inspiration to all those around them. However, it is no longer acceptable to many Māori that success at school in one's own country should come at the cost of their own language and culture.

Notwithstanding the success stories associated with many schools that are driven by a strong tikanga Māori orientation, there is a sizeable group of Māori children and adolescents whose parents and whānau are unable to pass on to them their language and culture and who have missed the opportunity of experiencing education within a context of Te Ao Māori and have tasted little success in the mainstream environment. Part of this group consists of students who are often frustrated by school, and sometimes uncertain about where they stand in terms of their ethnicity. The diversity of the Māori reality is such that some tamariki have either a working knowledge of or fluency in their language, and other tamariki have neither. Some embrace te reo and tikanga Māori; others, who have been isolated from it, may be prone to experience some paranoia when confronted with it (J. Macfarlane, 2003). Nonetheless, Durie (2001) contends that all groups have a right to a good quality of life, and to live as Māori. Schools and families need to be aware of this reality, and must play a role in shaping the behaviour of these students and in eliminating or reducing the frustrations and insecurities surrounding them.

It is important to establish where educational processes are succeeding for these young people, and to examine the social and cultural contexts of their life experiences. Behaviour always occurs within a cultural and community context. Yet many Māori students live their lives in cultural and community contexts that are quite different from those of the school and the mainstream community. Beane (1997) and Ladson-Billings (1995) explain how such contexts are important for understanding and helping students who are experiencing difficulties at school. Peterson and Ishii-Jordan (1994), however, propose that there is still a dearth of information on how and through what processes these cultural contexts are "listened" to by mainstream teachers.

Lack of progress of Māori students in mainstream schools has been attributed to many sources. Some older Māori retain the memory of their own schooling, in which they were told not to use their own language (Walker, 1991), and were put down as an inferior society practising an inferior culture. Some of their children are now themselves parents, and have little language or cultural knowledge to pass on to their own children. These experiences can be compared with the plight of the native Americans (Kallam, Hoernicke, and Coser, 1994), descended from several generations of a semi-assimilated minority, whose sense of loss translated into a deep suspicion on their part of the majority culture-based agencies.

A lack of understanding of Māori customs on the part of the dominant New Zealand culture may be one critical reason why many Māori students fail in mainstream educational settings and are often excluded from it. In a society which is frequently described as bicultural or multicultural, it is not surprising that individual underachievement is often "explained" by referring to perceived deficits within the individual's cultural background. However, it is increasingly common to hear the demand that "the style of content of service delivery in such areas as health, social welfare, and education should be constructed so as to take account of the cultural background of the people receiving these services, or that the service should be culturally appropriate" (Morrisey, 1997, p. 93). This may well be the plea of some educators: that it is time to listen to culture.

CHAPTER TWO

Listening to culture

The need to "listen to culture" has received considerable attention from New Zealand researchers (Bishop and Glynn, 1999; Clark et al., 1996; Glynn, 1997; Hohepa, 1999; Macfarlane, 2000a; Macfarlane, Glynn, Presland, and Greening, 2000; Penetito, 1996; Smith, 1992; Smith, 1999). They have emphasised that schools should be models not only for the expression of respect for cultural difference, but also for power sharing. Hardman, Drew, and Egan (1999) contend that at school, young people's thoughts and feelings about diverse cultures are at least partially shaped by what they learn in the classroom. Incomplete information, stereotypical presentations about different cultures, or lack of full participation of minority groups in the classroom detract from gaining understanding or appreciation about cultures that characterise New Zealand. Neglectful or careless treatment of this important topic has the potential to perpetuate eurocentric notions and to relegate the tangata-whenua (people of the land, indigenous people) to the status of an "outsider" position, along with the numerous minority ethnic groups who have arrived in New Zealand since the signing of the Treaty of Waitangi. A more complete education, according to Hardman et al. (1999), must include recognition of the role of the cultures, and in particular the role of tangata-whenua, in shaping knowledge bases and pedagogies within educational programmes, while fostering attitudes of respect and appreciation.

Teaching strategies that are more inclusive, collaborative, and allow for reciprocal teaching and learning also need to be adopted in classrooms. These strategies provide strong opportunities for power sharing. Contemporary multicultural education promotes recognition and respect for differences and diversity (Kitano, 1997). Contemporary general education has a long way to go in this respect. Contemporary special education, in contrast, does tend to focus on individual needs, strengths, and preferences. However, the notion of "special education" as distinct and different from general education is being increasingly challenged (Brown, 2002).

Failure to succeed in mainstream classroom instruction has often been associated with Māori students, yet a contrasting and positive picture is presented by Bevan-Brown (1999). While Gollnick and Chinn (1994) noted that programmes for the gifted and talented in North America seem to have fewer of the minority cultures represented, Bevan-Brown reports that Māori have a much more holistic view of human development in general, and this holistic perception reflects Māori values, customs, and beliefs. Moltzen (cited in Fraser, Moltzen, and Ryba, 2000) refers to Bevan-Brown's research, in which she found that the Māori concept of special abilities is broad and wide-ranging, with importance placed on both qualities and abilities. These include service to Māoridom, Māori knowledge, spirituality, language, musical, literary and artistic ability, aesthetic appreciation, leadership, sporting prowess, intelligence, knowledge and appreciation of nature, and qualities such as patience, humility, bravery, and sensitivity to others. Bevan-Brown also argues that many Māori students who present with challenging behaviours may also present with special abilities, through mana tinana, manaaki, and aroha or other such qualities, which may not even be identified or acknowledged. Bevan-Brown seems to be suggesting that "not listening to culture" has the potential to mar teacher, student, and parent relationships. Among the problems facing New Zealand education, probably none is more pervasive, persistent, or pressing than learning how to teach children whose attempts at learning result in failure, and whose behaviour exacerbates inharmonious relationships.

A number of theoretical models have been developed by some of the most influential international educational thinkers of the past half-century. However, in all the theories underpinning these models, little attention is paid to cultural and ethnic factors. Yet it is often claimed that theories provide the conceptual framework that channels the action or interventions which are introduced (Walker and Shea, 1999).

> One form of intervention, carried out within two different conceptual frameworks, can have radically different meanings and lead to radically different experiences and outcomes for the participants (Rhodes and Tracy, pp. 23–24: cited in Walker and Shea, 1999).

Walker and Shea (1999) propose that if Rhodes and Tracy are correct, then educators' perceptions of children and of their behaviour will largely determine the behaviour management interventions selected and imposed. The significance of this is that if school systems are designed to serve the majority, then the minority are liable to be marginalised. When a mainstream education system does not satisfactorily accommodate diversity, the system must be deemed inadequate, and modifications are required (Hardman et al., 1999). Behavioural interventions based on western theories and their respective strategies have not altogether succeeded in New Zealand schools, particularly when it comes to changing the behaviour of Māori students needing help.

Recent developments in New Zealand special education, such as the Specialist Education Services (SES)[1] Special Education 2000 policy (SE2000), and the Resource Teachers Learning and Behaviour (RTLB) national professional development programme, have, to varying degrees, recognised that Māori and bicultural issues are a high priority in the training of special education personnel. The platform for this has been the Treaty of Waitangi. The Treaty now occupies an important position of providing guiding principles for much of the recent legislation, government policy, and administrative practices.

The Treaty has particular implications for education, at all levels and in all activities (Glynn, 1998). Article 1 established that there are two Treaty partners who share responsibility for shaping the direction of New Zealand, in all arenas, including the development of policy in general education and special education. Article 2 established that while Māori ceded administrative control (kāwanatanga) to the colonial government, they retained their autonomy (tino rangatiratanga) over defining, promoting, and protecting their own treasures (taonga). Included among these treasures are language, knowledge, and the transmission of knowledge. In other words, Article 2 concerns the rights of Māori to define and promote their own curriculum and determine appropriate pedagogy. Article 3 ensures equitable access to the educational resources of the state, and the right to expect equity of educational outcomes for Māori students. A programme for behaviour intervention in New Zealand should address all articles of the Treaty of Waitangi, especially those of power sharing through the recognition of Māori autonomy. This will need to be visible in terms of personnel delivering the intervention programme, and needs to take

---

[1] Group Special Education (GSE) is a newly formed group in the Ministry of Education. GSE focuses on providing services—directly or indirectly—to children and young people with special education needs. On 28 February 2002 Specialist Education Services (SES) combined with the Ministry of Education.

into account the content of the programme, and the manner in which it is delivered (Glynn, 1998).

Indigenous peoples throughout the world have sustained their unique worldviews and associated knowledge systems for hundreds of years. These cultures have exhibited remarkable durability in the face of major social upheavals taking place as a result of transformative colonising forces beyond their control. Kawagley and Barnhardt (1997) contend that many of the core values, beliefs, and practices associated with these worldviews have survived, and are being recognised as having an adaptive integrity that is as valid for today's generation as it was for generations past. The depth of indigenous knowledge, Māori knowledge, rooted in the long inhabitation of Hawaiki and Aotearoa offers benefits for all peoples, from curricular designer to consultant, from classroom teacher to teacher educator, as they search for more satisfying and sustainable ways to live in a society of diverse cultures and ethnicities.

The following chapters attempt to report on the culturally responsive pedagogy of an Enrichment Class for Māori students. They show, from within a Māori worldview, how a better understanding of the experiences of disaffected Māori students in mainstream education can be achieved, and, ultimately, more effective ways of improving the achievement of these students can be promoted.

Improving school experiences and achievement for Māori students is increasingly understood to depend on the pedagogical skills and integrity of classroom teachers. Hilliard (cited in Ford, Obiakor, and Patton, 1995) contends that the historically oppressive treatment of culture is at the base of difficulties in some aspects of professional practice. The cultural reality of Māori people remains strong. The culture is there. It is vital. It is meaningful. But, according to Hilliard, one must be in a position to observe it. This requires assisting all teachers in mainstream education to "listen to culture" (Macfarlane, 2000a). This book will describe how calculated, pervasive, and deliberate connections to Māori epistemology formed the core of the learning activities at the Enrichment Class, located within a mainstream primary school.

CHAPTER THREE

Ngongotahā School and the Ngāti-Whakaue Enrichment Class

Ngongotahā Primary School is situated at the northern base of Mount Ngongotahā, with Lake Rotorua to the east and the Mamaku ranges to the west. The school's location gives it a natural and direct connection to the Ngāti Rangiwewehi tribe, as well as to Ngāti Whakaue. The school has maintained a roll of around 400 for a number of years. On average, 60 percent of the students are Māori. As a mainstream primary school in a moderately populated suburb of Rotorua, like other state schools in New Zealand, its charter has to include the requirements of both the National Education Guidelines (NEGs) and the communities the school serves, as well as the National Administration Guidelines (NAGs). The school principal, Terry Morrison, is considered by many local and national educationalists to be one of the most astute visionaries in the profession. In 1998 Mr Morrison was appointed by the Ministers of Education and Māori Development to the Māori Education Commission, an entity of six Māori educators charged with collaboratively consulting with the Māori education and tribal communities to advocate for structures that would advance achievement for Māori children (Te Puni Kokiri, 1998).

The classroom, the Ngāti-Whakaue Enrichment Class, has a special function.[2] It was a Māori-controlled initiative, with an emphasis on improving the literacy and numeracy of the students it served. The class's tino rangatiratanga (autonomous Māori cultural status) arose from its being funded by the Ngāti-Whakaue Education Endowment Trust. Ngāti-Whakaue is a hapū of the Te

---

[2] The Ngāti-Whakaue Enrichment Class continues its operation as an integral part of Ngongotahā School. The unit is still being resourced by the Ngāti-Whakaue Education Endowment Trust.

Arawa tribe. The Ngāti-Whakaue Endowment Trust Board was created in 1995, its core purpose being to apply the tribe's net revenue for the general purpose of education. The Trust's mission is:

> To enhance the legacy of Ngāti-Whakaue tipuna by the responsible and effective management of the endowment and the provision of financial support to the beneficiaries of the Trust for educational purposes that adds value and benefit to the community.

The successful application by Ngongotahā School for funding enabled the literacy and numeracy Enrichment Class to be established. The innovational and administrative skills of Gaye Ruru, the assistant principal at the time, were critical factors in the establishment of the programme, and Mrs Ruru retained mentorship of the programme's operations throughout its tenure. In addition, Gaye Ruru was responsible for the overall operation of the Ngāti-Whakaue class. In many respects, the establishment of the class was ignited by her concern for the difficulties being experienced by Māori children in acquiring and retaining literacy and numeracy skills. The following statements are taken from a focused discussion with Gaye Ruru in May 2000 and these reflect some of her thinking and philosophies:

> I was concerned with literacy, numeracy, and behaviour. We have worked very hard to get Māori parents here taking part in things, and time and time again this has been frustrating . . .

> So, the observations I made showed a number of issues at stake. These included parent support, children's learning, and behaviour modification. I am strong in the belief that learning and academic engagement should be always at the forefront. If a child has a behaviour difficulty, I first want to find out what is happening academically for that child in that classroom. That is what is important. Then if behaviour is still an issue, it's only a smaller part of a big picture . . .

> What we are trying to do is optimise these children's chances of being stronger through the rest of their lives, not just improvement in the here and now. Ideally, what I would like would be that there would be one or two teachers that these children will remember when they are adults, and that this will come from the opportunities that present themselves to them now. These memories will stay with them through their lives, the memories of Ngongotahā School and the Ngāti-Whakaue class.

Gaye Ruru was determined that there had to be cultural compatibility between the teacher and the students in the Ngāti-Whakaue Enrichment Class. That teacher also had to be experienced and competent in carrying out assessments and planning programmes that would improve the educational achievements of young Māori students who were struggling in regular classrooms.

Gaye Ruru also raised the issue of the need to provide professional development for teachers, as a means to improving their competence in working with Māori students and their whānau. She believed that providing professional development for teachers would be preferable to "leaving it to the expert". She saw this approach as a better way of utilising the skills of experienced and competent teachers, and she had an individual in mind who possessed those skills: Bev Anaru (see next chapter).

From the outset, she was certain that Bev Anaru would be the person who would be best to set up and run the Ngāti-Whakaue class, as well as the functions that the class would serve:

> I knew the person had to be an experienced teacher, and one of the criteria I always have in anything I set up is, if it's not going to be quality, don't start it. And I knew that person who had these qualities. I've had the advantage of three and a half years of Bev Anaru working in a regular class at this school, and Bev is a marvellous person for advancing information. I'd give her stuff to read and the next thing she'd be straight back having a brainstorm with me about what she could do in the room, so I knew that she would make it work in the ways that we wanted it to work.

What did they want? The management and staff of Ngongotahā School were determined to address the low educational achievement of a large number of (mainly Māori) students in literacy and numeracy, through high-quality teaching and learning strategies. Analysis of the results of three School Entry Assessment (SEA) tests (Ministry of Education, 1997b), regularly carried out for all new or early entrants at Ngongotahā School (Concepts About Print, Tell Me/Ki Mai, and Checkout/Rapua) matched the New Zealand-wide results: non-Māori regularly scored significantly higher than Māori on all three. Table 3.1 outlines the disparities in the results.

As well as responding to the SEA results with regard to literacy and numeracy, the school leaders saw it as critical to address students' emotional and social development as well. Two fundamental aspects drove this approach. First, Māori concepts, values, and practices were to be continually modelled, taught, and reinforced. Secondly, this mainstream school and its special programme would continue to strive to work in partnership with its Māori community. It

Table 3.1

Disparities between Māori and non-Māori achievement in School Entry Assessment test results at Ngongotahā School

Test	Non-Māori average	Māori average
Checkout	21.3	13.7
Concepts About Print	12.9	7.4
Tell Me	14.2	11.0

(Ruru, 2001)

aimed to achieve five pivotal outcomes:

- higher attainment by students in literacy and numeracy;
- increased involvement of Māori parents in the process and direction of their children's education;
- improved self-esteem in children and parents;
- improved study skills in children and an increased understanding of lifelong learning for parents; and
- greatly improved cultural identity for Māori students.

The Enrichment Class programme was described in the school charter as an activity-based, child-centred developmental programme encapsulating the seven essential learning areas of the New Zealand Curriculum Framework, along with the eight essential skills (Ministry of Education, 1993). There was particular emphasis given to literacy and numeracy and the associated processes of communication, co-operation, and problem solving. The daily programme consisted of the activities outlined in Table 3.2.

The school charter proclaimed that the over-arching dimension of the programme was a spiritual one, that of Māori tikanga and wairua. The project's organisers and providers were emphatic that the authentic presence of Māoritanga in the programme was a source of strength and possibility, to the extent that it replaced notions of deficit and disaffection.

The project employed Beverley (Bev) Anaru as its director. Affiliating to the Ngāti Awa and Ngai Tuhoe tribes of the Eastern Bay of Plenty region, she has close affiliations to the iwi of Ngāti-Whakaue through her husband, Peter. She is a former principal, Teachers College lecturer, and Regional Education Board Adviser. While these credentials presented her as highly suitable to carry forward the role and purpose of the project, it was her reputation as a classroom artiste or orchestrator of classroom activities (Eisner, 1994), that distinguished her. The criteria for appointing Anaru as head teacher of the

Table 3.2

Daily programme of the Ngāti-Whakaue Enrichment Class at Ngongotahā School

Programme focus	Daily expectations
• News Book: oral language, current events, pupil/ teacher sharing session, modelled story, guided story writing • Mathematics: maintenance (looking back, revising), in depth teaching • Focus of the lesson: teaching, modelling, sharing, practice, manipulating equipment, recording, self-evaluation, reinforcement • Reading: independent reading of carefully selected "easy" level books, alphabet/letter link activities, teacher reading to children, guided reading session with teacher • Story Writing: developing writing independence through modelling of the use of punctuation, use of alphabet/letter sound charts, word resources available, rehearsing story orally, reading completed story with teacher • Make and Do: self-chosen creative art-type activity	• Read to the teacher • Write a story • Read a chosen book from their level box • Listen to a story read by a teacher • Share a comment with someone during sharing time • Be a monitor for a selected duty • Enjoy "make and do" time • Be noticed as a VIP some time during the day

(Anaru, 2001)

Ngāti-Whakaue class included her leadership and teaching skills, her ability to reach outwards to the community, and to attract parents into the school, and her cultural competence.

CHAPTER FOUR

Culturally responsive teaching and the Bev Anaru factor

I was alerted to Bev Anaru's teaching process and in February 2000 I approached the administrators of Ngongotahā School regarding my interest in undertaking a study of the Ngāti-Whakaue Enrichment Class. Once affirmed, I commenced the research activities between March and June of that year visiting the site either one or two mornings per week.

The research protocols (interviews and observations) were complemented by frequently using field notes to provide more in-depth background and to clarify classroom activities and interactions. The field notes contained descriptions of what was being observed and stated. The date and time of the observations were recorded, and everything I believed to be worth noting was included. The use of technological tools, such as audio recorder and video camera made the collection of field notes more efficient and the notes themselves more comprehensive. In this study, the types of information sources included:

- The setting – the physical environment within which the programme took place: this included space and objects in the environment.
- The human, social environment – the ways in which people in the programmes interacted and behaved toward each other. The perceptions of parents and significant others were also important.
- Programme implementation activities – What goes on in the programme? What do various people actually do? How are resources allocated?
- The vernacular of the programme – different organisations have their own language or jargon to describe the encounters they experience in their work:

capturing the vernacular was an important way to record how people in the programme understood their experiences.

- Communication – verbal and non-verbal cues about what was happening in the programme: the way people present themselves, express their opinions, and share their feelings.

Two separate groups of students, all of whom were Māori, were enrolled into the unit. Group 1 consisted of 10 Year 1 students and Group 2 consisted of 12 Year 2 students. Similarities between the two groups in terms of their structure and design convinced me that a study of one of the groups would provide sufficient data from which to draw firm conclusions. I opted to study the latter group. The students on the programme had been identified as having learning and behaviour difficulties. They were withdrawn from their regular classrooms to attend the Ngāti-Whakaue Enrichment Class for three morning sessions each week, for a minimum period of two terms and a maximum of a full year. The morning sessions were for an intensive $1^1/_2$ hours. The children were tutored in a wānanga (a place for Māori learning) type classroom. Two paraprofessionals (Māori women from the local community) worked with individual children while Bev Anaru attended to the larger group. The larger group worked on the mat initially, moving to tables after Bev was satisfied that a reasonable level of readiness (for progressing the concepts under scrutiny) had been attained.

In the early stages of the research I was able to link the pedagogy of the Ngāti-Whakaue Enrichment Class with some of the recognised literature on good classroom management. The classroom had a busy "tone" to it. Anaru's approach was very much in line with Jacob Kounin's (1977) central focus of classroom management. She was well organised, and each lesson was presented with precision, clarity, and exuberance. Room management provided for movement to "work the crowd" (Jones, 1987) and allowed for attention to be given to all students simultaneously. Anaru's trait of "withitness" (Kounin, 1977), enabled her to know what was going on in all parts of the classroom at all times. The classroom was bright: rules of the classroom were displayed, as were examples of children's work, awards, reminders, class timetables, and pictures promoting the bicultural nature of the Ngāti-Whakaue region. Māori translations of key concepts and words were evident on walls, tables, and charts. The room had a "texture" which incorporated real sight, sound, smell, and taste. Importantly, the students seemed to delight in being there, in the presence of a skilled practitioner, who valued each of them for simply being who they were. Children reputed to have behaviour problems did not misbehave. Most were said to have learning difficulties, yet in this environment they were motivated to achieve better, and records of their progress attested to that. So-called withdrawn children became vocal contributors, and impulsive children seemed more in control of themselves.

Bev Anaru has a rich store of situated knowledge, both of the New Zealand national curriculum, and of te reo and tikanga Māori. She has been at the cutting edge of knowing and learning about curriculum content, classroom and social processes, academic tasks, and students' understandings. Her teaching style manifested the principles inherent both in Kounin's (1977) Instructional Management Approach and in the Hikairo Rationale (Macfarlane, 1997). Anaru's lessons had good momentum, in getting the students to attend to the tasks in hand, getting on with it, getting on with them (building and maintaining relationships), and getting closure, before a smooth transition to the next activity was executed (Smith and Laslett, 1993). Her demeanour had a powerful influence on her students' learning and behaviour, her posture displaying confidence and suggesting leadership, enthusiasm, enjoyment, and appreciation of the content of the learning experiences and of the context in which this was taking place. The children respected Bev Anaru's assertive, no-nonsense approach. Their engagement in learning and the delight they showed in "being around her" created opportunities for their teacher to smile warmly, a trait identified by Pierce (1996) as simple yet significant in terms of building trust between learner and teacher.

Group alerting, or systems for gaining attention and clarifying expectations, played an important part in Anaru's approach. Her tactics included a range of Fredric Jones' (cited in Charles, 1999) uses of body language to help students pay attention and stay on task. Anaru was often observed using non-verbal behaviour management strategies, such as eye contact, physical proximity, conversational pause, facial expressions, and gestures in classroom interactions with students.

An excerpt from a national newspaper (Lose, 2000) captured something of Anaru's teaching style. Headed "Beverley lives for teaching", the article paid tribute to her receiving a Multi Serve National Education Service Award. The newspaper report quoted Anaru: "There is nothing like teaching a child to read and write . . . money can't buy the joy you get from seeing the glint in the youngster's eye when they make out their first words . . . But there is one other ingredient for educational success – aroha."

When asked about her initial involvement with the Ngāti-Whakaue class, it was clear that Anaru's primary intention was to make a difference to the learning experiences and achievements of the children. She declared that, given the stage she was at in her career, she wanted to "give something back to the profession". Bev Anaru was adamant that her pedagogical approach responded to the special learning needs of the children, through positive relationships and classroom climate. A core element was instilling in the students a pride in themselves, a belief in themselves, and a realisation on their part that to be Māori was a dimension to be celebrated.

Anaru expressed great concern about the inability of many teachers to develop an awareness of children's ethnic socialisation, and how this socialisation affects how children think, feel, and act (Phinney and Rotheram, 1987). She referred to ethnic socialisation as one's roots. Quite often, during our conversations, she would talk about "her roots":

> I think my approach to education, to life for that matter, has been guided by an appreciation of my culture, my roots. I am lucky, I had experiences in two worlds all my life. My Scottish father and Māori mother, one Presbyterian, the other Ringatū. My mother was a powerful woman. I remember the long conversations she had with John Rangihau, particularly at the time John was first appointed Māori Welfare Officer for the Whakatane area. As a teacher she obviously had some knowledge of learning processes. She also took her Māoritanga with her into the classroom, on to the playground, and to the staffroom. (Personal communication, April 2000)

Bev Anaru modelled the behaviour and values she desired from the students. During our discussions, she talked about the bonding she was able to create with her students and former students. She talked about a "belonging", as opposed to "the wall":

> Over many years I have been both rapt and frustrated. I am rapt when I see really good teaching of Māori students and frustrated when teachers put this wall up between them and their students . . . especially non-Māori teachers with Māori students . . . worried about subject rather than student. Don't get me wrong, the content of my class presentations is important . . . absolutely, but the mana of self-affirming of the children comes first. I love being there. Better still, the kids know I love being there. (Personal communication, April 2000)

Hilty (cited in Franklin, 1998) asked "What has love got to do with it? All teachers love children, right?" For many teachers this is true, up to a point.

The day-to-day challenge of teaching children with special education needs might be exciting, but for teachers like Bev Anaru it is love that keeps giving them hope, socially and educationally. More importantly, for many students, this bonding with a particular teacher may mark their first and most significant positive interaction in a school setting. Hilty contends that while love and a sense of mission are seldom discussed in conjunction with school failure, they seem to play a role in the lives of teachers who elect to teach children who are "dismissed", figuratively and literally, from many schools. Love and care, referred to in Chapter Eight as manaakitanga, initiate a dialogue that lays the foundation for a successful and reciprocal teaching and learning experience.

CHAPTER FIVE

Messages from parents . . . and a child

The setting up of the Ngāti-Whakaue Enrichment Unit was from the outset intended actively to involve parents in the programme. In an article published in Reading Forum (2001) the Assistant Principal, Gaye Ruru, outlined five specific ways that parents and whānau were to be involved:

- Parents and whānau would be involved in the progress their children were making.
- They would be encouraged to offer assistance to the programme both in and out of the classroom.
- They would be expected to share with their children what the learning goals were, including participating in the regular review of the goals.
- They would be expected to attend two Open Days per term, and as well they would be encouraged to maintain regular ongoing contact with the leader, Bev Anaru.
- The staff of the unit would endeavour to instil in the parents and whānau a lifelong interest in their children's education.

The value and energy of community partnerships at Ngongotahā School as a whole, and the Enrichment Class in particular, went in two directions. The school was not about just asking the community to help it and thereby add to the school's resources. The school was adamant about giving something in return. The Ngongotahā School leaders looked at different groups in the community and considered how they were serving them, and what links they had to the school.

Much of the literature on best practice is founded on a growing awareness that parents play a crucial role in facilitating and maintaining developmental and cognitive gains in young children who have special education needs (McKinley, 2002). The closer the parent moves towards full involvement in the education of their child, the more potential impact there is on the child's educational achievement. Parental participation is related to significant academic progress; fewer discipline problems; increased self-esteem and social skills; and better school attendance, study habits, and attitudes towards school (Henderson, 1987). From focused discussions with the parents and whānau of the Ngāti-Whakaue Enrichment Class, the parents' participation contributed to gains in the children's achievement.

The account which follows was constructed from two sets of discussions with parents of students of the Enrichment Class, after invitations were sent to parents by Bev Anaru. The first discussion was in the form of an informal chat with the parents, during the course of an "open morning". Parents were invited to attend the unit and to observe and participate in the activities. Ten parents attended this "open morning", a most satisfactory percentage given that one parent had two children in the Enrichment Class. This was a good opportunity for me to get to introduce myself to the parents, and to talk to them about the nature of my work generally, and the role I was carrying out as a university researcher specifically. In the course of this "small talk", the parents and I were often able to make connections, particularly since I was able to whakapapa (show a tribal link) to the whānau and the hapū (sub-tribe) of Ngāti-Whakaue and Ngāti Rangiwewehi. When parents found out that I was indeed "one of them", their perceptions of this university researcher changed. Personal identity and tribal identity (connectedness) took on more importance than professional identity. In Māoridom, small talk is important talk – so important that dignity and integrity play a large role in ethical behaviour. The notion of integrity here refers to respecting others' views in the course of communicating. At this "open day" of the Ngāti-Whakaue unit, some exchanging of views took place between myself and the parents individually. When they were invited to participate in a focus discussion as a group of parents, this was greeted with enthusiasm, and most chose to participate.

Gudykunst (1994) contends that the term "communication" refers to the exchange of messages and the creation of meaning. Although many of the parents had imparted their respective views on the activities of the Ngāti-Whakaue unit and the progress their children were making there, I was keen to assign more significance to their messages in a hui, in this case a semi-formal, focused discussion forum.

Eight parents attended this second hui. They found the whole idea of a "formal" discussion about their children's educational environment (the Ngāti-Whakaue unit) to be rather curious, yet they were enthusiastic about taking part. At the beginning of the meeting, I recited a karakia (prayer) and presented a brief mihi (greeting) to the group. A series of open-ended questions followed. These covered: the learning environment; the programme; the classroom organisation; the benefits that accrue to their children by way of their being enrolled in the programme; the mana of the teacher and whether the teacher and the teaching had resulted in positive changes in the children's learning and behaviour; the presence of tikanga Māori in the programme; and their thoughts on how the programme might be improved. When the tapes of the interview were transcribed, it was readily obvious that there was significant congruence in the responses to the questions. Consequently, it was possible to economise by analysing the responses of five, rather than all eight parents. This approach was carried out without any dissonance to the interpretation of the data, nor any disrespect to the other three parents (real names are not used).

The environment

Question: How would you describe the learning environment of the Ngāti-Whakaue Enrichment Class?

It is very comfortable for the children. The learning activities are exciting (Helen).

Yes, I agree. The children develop confidence there. I would say that it is very good for children to build their confidence. I've noticed that with mine (her child). From someone who had no confidence at school, now can't wait to get to school (Nola).

My son was like that, now he loves going to school. I think it is a confidence thing. And they learn the skills too. The improvement in reading and writing has been amazing (Jen).

Yes. I agree. They are taught the skills, the basics. She (Bev Anaru) goes right back to the basics and teaches the skills…so skilfully. But there's a lot of praise for the children (from Bev Anaru). The learning is focused on fun. There is just so much respect for each individual child and every child has potential (Jan).

My daughter was the biggest bully out…she didn't like school, had heaps of problems learning things. So the environment is comfortable for her and she has got a lot of confidence now. As they (the others) said…back to the basics. Now she's doing well (Ben).

Descriptions of the classroom environment varied. Helen saw the classroom as comfortable and exciting. Nola agreed, and added that for her, the environment was such that it built confidence in her child in such a way that going to school now had a certain appeal, suggesting that her child's former school experiences were rather uninviting ones. Jen also said that her son now loved going to school, and mentioned the amazing progress he had made in literacy and numeracy. In addition, according to Jan, the skills taught to the children were taught skilfully. Ben was impressed with the improvement in both learning and behaviour made by his daughter on account of being in this classroom.

A warm and inviting climate seems to describe aptly the psychological and social dynamics. The dynamics of the classroom are influenced by certain student factors and certain teacher factors. The psychological atmosphere of any classroom depends in great part on the teacher factors, including disposition, competencies and skills, and actions. According to Smith, Polloway, Patton, and Dowdy (2001), a teacher's attitude toward students with special needs can dramatically affect the quality of education that a student will receive during the time he or she is in that teacher's classroom. The parents' responses suggested that such an atmosphere existed in the Ngāti-Whakaue unit. For their children, it created a supportive, safe, comfortable environment in which Māori students with learning difficulties were able to learn without fear of being ridiculed or threatened.

The programme

Question: What do you believe is the most important aspect of the programme?

It's how she covers the different areas of the curriculum. Bev does it with such good organisation (Jan).

She seems to have it all worked out in her head what she wants to do, very organised. There is quite a bit of order . . . but at the right moment if a kid says something or does something she will give attention to that . . . sort of issue . . . and she uses it as a teaching point. She recognises what all the children are doing all the time yet can still focus her attention on one child . . . without ignoring the others (Nola).

The important thing that I see about the programme is Bev. It's how she leads the class without being harsh. The kids love her (Jen).

It is how it is organised and how the children get a lot of attention. I think having a small class allows her to do that and it's been great . . . for my kids . . . for all the kids really (Helen).

What's important is the class atmosphere and the organisation. My daughter has improved because of the organisation. Now she knows what to do because everything is so clear. Nothing is sort of rushed into. Her learning is better . . . and her behaviour (Ben).

Yes, it's the amount of learning and how children have fun and learn at the same time (Helen).

That's the sort of mixture that you see in the class all the time – fun and learning. Even though it's fun Mrs Anaru is always in control at the same time (Nola).

Parents cited good organisation, attending to the students, and the mixture of learning and fun as some of the most important aspects of the programme. The literature is explicit that the effective teacher is organised. The general curriculum documents and programmes of lessons (for a day, week, or term) were usually designed by the teaching team and were always appropriate to the age and abilities of the students.

Two characteristics identified in classic classroom management research (Kounin, 1977) consider a teacher's ability to manage classrooms effectively by implementing strategies referred to as "withitness", where the teacher has an overall awareness of what is happening in the classroom, and "overlapping", where the teacher has the ability to deal with more than one event simultaneously. These teacher behaviours did not go unnoticed by the parents, and nor did the element of fun and learning. Glasser (1993) claims that most misbehaviour occurs because students are bored or frustrated by school experiences. Glasser maintains that if schools are to survive, they must be redesigned to emphasise quality in all students' work. They must no longer attempt to coerce students, a tactic that is clearly ineffective. Instead, teachers must lead students deeply into learning that addresses what is important in students' lives.

Bev Anaru regularly infused her Māori students' lived experiences into her teaching. In a maths lesson, she was heard to say: "Hamish, your koroua (grandfather) and kuia (grandmother) have twelve mokopuna, tika tena? (is that right?)" She then proceeded to ask others in the class about how many mokopuna there were in their whānau. This led to looking at mathematical concepts of addition. She used effective questions which were clear and brief, and identified the aspects to which the children were expected to respond. As an example, she asked, "What do you notice about the structure of Arawhata's whānau?" "Why do your koroua and kuia go for a hui at the marae?" "Think about the number of buildings on the marae you go to. Add these up. Tell me about the purpose of the buildings." "What is the purpose of the koha (gift offered at hui to help hosts)?" "Let's try to work out the cost of a small hui at Arawhata's marae, for 20 manuhiri (visitors) and five tangata-whenua (hosts)." Thus Anaru showed an understanding of the family and cultural contexts from which the students came, and how this understanding could be closely related to the lesson objectives, or the expected outcomes for the study.

Respect, consistency, modelling, expectations

Question: In what ways do Mrs Anaru and her team (two paraprofessionals) show that classroom organisation, and good planning, and respect, are important?

It's how they show respect for the kids and how the kids respect them back. There is never, never a negative word spoken towards any of the children. The teachers are so positive. I think they show it by always being positive (Nola).

That's right too. I think they show this by encouragement in the first place. It's always encouraging the kids – the three teachers are such good role models that the children are now believing in themselves. The other thing that I think happens is that the teachers encourage the children to own their actions and activities. They put the onus back on the children to perform (Jan).

They show the kids what to do in a good way…it's clear to the children what they (the children) have to do in the class, with their work and that. In other classes I'm sure many kids find it hard to understand what they have to do, and get confused. But not with Mrs Anaru, and the other two teachers as well. I agree that they really do encourage them a lot (Ben).

They (the teachers) have good expectations for these children. They really want the children to succeed and there are ways of rewarding them. They tell the kids how special they are, all the time, and awards are given to all the children (Jen).

They (the teachers) are consistent . . . they are not up and down. It seems that all of the children know what to do, or what is expected of them and they're not scared to have a go at anything. There is no such thing as "failure" in the class and that's . . . well . . . really something (Helen).

Respect, consistency, modelling, and having high expectations of the children are the key elements of teachers' behaviour that were noticed by the parents. Having high and realistic expectations for all students is a high order instructional principle. Bennett (1995) argues that high expectations are a necessary prerequisite for culturally fair education. But it is not only the teacher who needs to have high expectations for the students; students also need to have high expectations for themselves. The teachers in the Ngāti-Whakaue unit conveyed a sense of positive expectations for individual and group achievement. Bennett adds that this is especially important for those students whose lives have been surrounded by failure, and who have had conveyed to them little hope for success in school. Anaru constantly insisted that Māori students with special educational needs need to "taste success" regularly.

The benefits for children

Question: What do you see as the benefits for your child in their attending this programme?

It's bettering their understanding of learning and improving the skills in reading and spelling. Going to the basic areas and starting to help the children to get better at those (Helen).

That's right . . . it's about building skills in reading, spelling and maths . . . and mapping like what they were doing this morning and the kids loving it. The other benefit is that it has built up my son's self-esteem. He has gained confidence and it is showing up in all areas of his schooling. The other factor is that one-to-one teaching that the teachers in the class are able to give the children. The working in small groups has really helped my son's personal development (Jan).

Learning the skills and being confident to speak up, to have a go at things (Jen).

To have a go. My daughter has picked up so much in her learning and confidence (Ben).

For mine it is the skills, the learning, the confidence. I mean, it's almost like seeing a different child. But there is that going to the basics and rote learning sometimes, repeating it until it sinks in. But the fun and attention and the learning are all going on at the same time (Nola).

Parents were adamant about the noticeable improvements in skills and attitudes in their children's work, and going back to the basics. This is in line with the recommendation of Reynolds and Birch (1988) that the curriculum should be developmentally appropriate (e.g., do not teach long division until students have mastered addition and subtraction). The teachers in the Ngāti-Whakaue unit did not become so focused on what the students had not learned that they became bogged down in remediation. They identified the gaps in the students' knowledge and then were selective about what they needed to learn. They focused on the most important content (in this case, literacy and numeracy – what the parents referred to as "the basics") for helping them catch up and start to master the skills.

The power of mana tangata

Question: Does your child discuss his/her experiences (in the enrichment class) at home?

It is quite amazing really. All the time it is talking about what went on, what was learned, what Mrs Anaru did and said (Jen).

Yes, that's a real talking point at our home. Wanting to involve me in her (his daughter's) experiences with Mrs Anaru and the other teachers as well. It's an ongoing discussion point and I reckon that just shows how much that class is doing for the kids. My daughter never talks about school like that but when it comes to this classroom it's a different story. She is excited about it. I think she is getting a lot from this recognition (Ben).

I get told all the time about how much he loves coming to the sessions. He can't wait to get there and turns up first thing in the morning. There is never a bad word spoken about the class. The class is just put up here (points to the ceiling) (Jan).

Yes they both (her children) do, and with great emotion. They love Mrs Anaru and speak of her all the time. They always talk about the exciting time they had. But they talk also about what they had learned and about what they are learning at the moment. They really tell me and show me how motivated they are to learn (Helen).

It's the same for me. In our household one of the main talking points is Mrs Anaru and what they did in Mrs Anaru's class (Nola).

Ka miharo te tangata ki te pono o tetahi atu means "one person will admire the integrity of another". What was happening in the classroom was the children admiring their teacher. To see their children talking about their classroom experiences at home was a new experience for those parents.

While instructional methodology is an important consideration, the view of teacher effectiveness emerging here comes from a different—yet complementary—perspective. One parent's remarks about her children declaring over and over that they loved Mrs Anaru and spoke of her all the time expressed the regular theme coming through from all parents. These observations represent the manifestation of mana, as described by Māori Marsden. Marsden (cited in King, 1975) refers to mana as "a vital force or

40

personal magnetism which, radiating from a person, elicits in the beholder a response of awe and respect" (p. 63). Barlow (1993) contends that in modern times, this term mana has taken on various meanings, including the power of the gods (mana atua), the power of ancestors (mana tipuna), the power of the land (mana whenua), and the power of the individual (mana tangata). While each of these realms has an important place in education, it is mana tangata that is deserving of special recognition. This is the power of the individual, according to his or her ability and effort to develop skill and to gain knowledge in particular areas. Barlow cites the example of "the skilled warrior acquiring mana through the arts of combat and warfare under the code of the law of Tamatauenga, the god of war, and of women having personal power in respect of their role in taking care of children and, on the marae, in welcoming and caring for visitors" (p. 62). Patterson (1992) links noble qualities (rangatira qualities) to Māori virtues of beauty, strength, courage, and open-handedness. The message in the proverb "My courage is noble courage – Toku toa he toa rangatira" makes much of the qualities of a chief, just as the Ngāti-Whakaue parents made much of the qualities of Bev Anaru.

The power of attachment

Question: What do you believe are the factors that help the teachers in their work in this programme?

To me there are a variety of factors. The children are tested and they don't fear the testing (Jan).

The children are set up to succeed, not to fail. I think the unit teachers have realistic expectations for these children in the class and they tell the children all the time that they are wonderful. But what helps the teachers in their work is that there is regular things happening, good structure and organisation. And there are not too many kids, the numbers are quite low and they can really get to know the kids and vice-versa (Nola).

They extend the children. There is variety in the programme as well as consistency. There is a variety of wall displays, so colourful, and written texts. I think the children feel that they know them and have access to them (Jan).

And the children feel they can trust the teachers. So there's no fear, no put-downs and the children are more keen to get on with working and improving all the time (Ben).

There are all of those things. That one-to-one teaching too, and the small groups.

The teachers are warm people. The kids will give Mrs Anaru hugs. Yes, Mrs Anaru does have expectations for the children to succeed and she lets them know. They do it for her as well as themselves (Jen).

The parents noticed how the teachers in the Ngāti-Whakaue Enrichment Class reinforced and formed close personal attachments with the students. Youngsters in many cultures use the secure base with the attachment figure to gain the support they need to adapt to the outside world. Taking the Ngāti-Whakaue unit to be the secure base and Bev Anaru to be the attachment figure, it has to be stated that cultural differences abound in the behavioural concepts of attachment, since adaptations are understood quite differently in different cultural contexts. In the United States, according to Rothbaum, Weisz, Pott, Miyake, and Morelli (2000), the major understanding of attachment is in terms of exploration, and adaptation primarily refers to individuation and autonomous mastery of the environment. In Māori society, however, the major understanding appears to be in terms of dependence, and adaptation refers to accommodation, loyalty, physical expressions of feelings, and ultimately independence (Penniman, 1986; Ritchie and Ritchie, 1983). Makereti (in Penniman, 1986) refers to the intense attention paid to the child by the mother. When a child was sad or distressed, this was hard for the Māori mother to bear. Makereti says that the mother would take the child in her arms and croon over it, singing oriori, or lullaby songs, to soothe it. Māori mothers had many of these songs, and some mothers composed their own, some being very beautiful and poetic. While the teaching observed in the Ngāti-Whakaue unit did not go to that extreme, Bev Anaru was uninhibited in terms of expression of her feelings for the students she taught. She would hug them and sing to them when the time was appropriate to do that. She used praise effectively, demonstrating this by specifying the particulars of a child's accomplishment, fostering endogenous attributions. Alderman (1999) cites, as an example of endogenous attributions, when students believe they expend effort on the task because they enjoy the task, and/or want to develop task-relevant skills.

According to Guerra, Attar, and Weissberg (1997), teachers who limit their interactions with students and provide little praise for on-task and good performance are not only missing out on vital opportunities to increase compliance and academic achievement, they are also sending a message to students that they are not valued. Recent research (Sleeter and Grant, 1999) indicates that teachers of low-income minority children tend to minimise interactions with these students, and provide less contingent praise. This can be especially harmful to students who are already undervalued by society, and who receive little contingent praise or have few positive interactions at home. This situation appears to occur more often when teachers come from a culture different from that of their students. Teachers who hold negative attitudes toward Māori and other indigenous students are not likely to be effective socialisation agents for them. Teachers with these dispositions toward minority group students may, in fact, consciously or unconsciously, fail to exercise their socialisation functions for these students. When such cases arise, Pollard (2002) asks who takes responsibility to see that minority children receive the socialisation that they need in the school setting.

A long-term solution might be to make sure that more Māori have access to the teaching profession. A more immediate solution might be to encourage New Zealand education policy makers to make sure that more non-Māori teachers have access to Māori and bicultural professional development programmes.

Changes in the children

Question: What has been the one significant change, if any, in your child as a result of their attending the Ngāti-Whakaue Enrichment Class?

The changes have been enormous. James and Rangi come home with achievements and the joy is there, it lights up their faces and their lives. The change has been their attitude and their learning. You know, we were thinking of moving from the district but as a result of their enrichment by going to the class we have decided not to move. The Enrichment Class and Bev Anaru have had an effect on Rangi and James, and on the family. We're not moving now. These kids love it too much and we love them being there (Helen).

As I said my daughter's behaviour was a problem. But the important change has been in her positive attitude (Ben).

I will put it down to change in confidence. Now I see positive, the change in my son has been that he is now more positive and confident (Jan).

Attitude and self-esteem. A lot of things really, but mainly self-esteem (Nola).

Learning and behaviour. Big improvements in both of those (Jen).

Bev Anaru often talked about the many conversations she had had in her long and diverse teaching career. Many of these conversations were about her success with "difficult to teach" students. Bev claims that sucess is about aroha, love and respect for the dignity of the child. Senge, Cambron-McCabe, Lucas, Smith, Dutton, and Kleiner (2001) are in accord with Bev's thinking when they claim that in daily practice, it's as simple as treating other people as you would want to be treated. Acknowledging people (adults and children) respects their dignity, just as to not acknowledge someone is to takahi te mana (trample on their dignity). Developing in students a strong sense of their own dignity will help them to grow up to be adults who can take risks, handle minor failures, and act in ways that respect other people's dignity. The parents used a variety of terms to describe the one significant change in their child as a result of their attending the Ngāti-Whakaue unit, but each of these descriptions was linked to the concept of dignity.

Improving the programme

Question: What do you think could be done to improve the programme?

How can you improve it? Perhaps anything can be improved but I think more people need to know about it so that others can improve what they do. So it can only be improved by helping others to improve (Nola).

It should be every day rather than three days a week (Jen).

I can't see that there needs to be any improvement. My children have excelled since being in Mrs Anaru's class (Helen).

There are a lot of other children out there that need help. It can be improved by having more classes like that (Ben).

Just keep the programme going to help enrich the learning process for many children in the future. This is a wonderful programme . . . (Jan).

Parents found it difficult to identify single elements of the programme that they thought could be improved upon. They appeared to be quite surprised that the matter was even raised. The parents showed perception, however, by wanting to have more learning centres like the Ngāti-Whakaue Enrichment Class, and some parents expressed the need for the professional development of other teachers. One parent in particular, Ben, saw the need for similar provision to be made for many other students, rather than the "fortunate few" in Bev Anaru's class.

For proponents of inclusive education, such notions may seem to come from left field. This study was not intended to argue the pros and cons of inclusive education as opposed to special programmes, or vice versa. It sought to explore both the fundamentals and intricacies of culturally relevant pedagogies, and Bev Anaru was central to this. Her guiding principles referred to the importance of seeing students as unique, as individual, as well as vital members of the whānau. Implicit in this recognition of individuality was a recognition that each student was also different from each other student; that they were a heterogeneous group with different needs. However, for Bev Anaru this principle went beyond a general acknowledgment of individuality to refer specifically to the other half of the duality, that of whānau. It is an affective dimension. She saw the students as whole people within a whole whānau (in this sense classroom) unit. Parents noticed Bev Anaru's enthusiasm for building up the inner person. Her consideration of students' sense of identity suggested an awareness of students' feelings and emotions that was not limited to awareness of students solely as learners of academic content, although academic content was important too. Parents recognised that their children in the Ngāti-Whakaue Enrichment Class certainly were being enriched, and they wished that other children could have similar opportunities.

Culture

Question: In what ways do the teachers in the Ngāti-Whakaue Enrichment Class teach and demonstrate cultural things?

Some of the teaching, or most of the teaching lessons include Māori words and names, the walls have Māori designs and proverbs put up. The proverbs are there to encourage the children and to encourage them to be proud of their culture. Mrs Anaru is a beautiful Māori person. By that I mean she is not shy to show aroha and to give aroha (Helen).

The kids are shown Māori artefacts. They are often spoken to in Māori, they sing Māori waiata (songs) (Nola).

Yes. They will say a Māori word then in English give the meaning. For example "Candace, your kuia (grandmother) is here." The children pick up what the Māori word means. The classroom is full of Māori words and slogans (Jen).

Emphasis is placed on pronunciation. That is the children are "hearing" the correct pronunciation of Māori – names, place names, and objects. Work is done on learning about Aotearoa (Jan).

It is cultural, totally (Ben).

This classroom of Māori students, mentored and taught by Māori adults successfully, together form a collective total that is distinguished by its "Māoriness". Sometimes talking in Māori, singing in Māori, thinking and acting in Māori, helped to make the curriculum relevant to the students' experiential backgrounds. Daily, the students were encouraged to be proud of their culture. Parents noted that in the Ngāti-Whakaue class, Māori cultural values and practices were strongly supported and promoted. In what might be described as a modest way, Bev Anaru was seen by parents and others as affirming for their children what Smith (1995, p. 22) refers to as "expressing Māori autonomy (tino rangatiratanga), Māori language and cultural aspirations and validity".

The final interview was with a non-Māori student, Sandra (not her real name), who was in Bev Anaru's regular classroom before the Ngāti-Whakaue Enrichment Class was established, and her mother. Although Sandra was no longer in Bev Anaru's class, she was often observed being near Bev Anaru, talking to her, and reporting to her about her experiences at home and at school, at every opportunity (before school and during the lunch break in particular). Sandra was asked to make some comments on the learner and teacher rapport that existed between her former teacher (Mrs Anaru), herself, and the other 34 children in the class that was previously taught by Bev Anaru.

> She cared for everyone. She made us work hard and the work was interesting. She was different to any teacher, anyone I know. Mrs Anaru says things with expression (Sandra).

> When she was in Mrs Anaru's class, she talked about their experiences all the time, on the weekends also. She wrote stories and addressed them to Mrs Anaru saying things like "You are a wonderful teacher". . . . "I like you" . . . In the mornings she would get off the bus, and whereas a lot of children will play, she will go straight to the classroom. I like her (Mrs Anaru's) teaching. And she likes all the other kids. She explains things a lot and can keep an audience. She captivates. On grandparents' day my father came with us and he was amazed at her energy, her ability to work the kids, keep their attention (Sandra's mum).

When Bev Anaru was principal of Te Teko School, the school was 100 per cent Māori. However, she has taught in schools with high non-Māori populations, and in schools overseas. Across these educational contexts, her passion and successes remained constant. Her ability to connect to the students appears to be the point of difference.

Culturally responsive teachers need not come from the same culture as the students. Giroux (1994, p. 30) claims that "pedagogy in the critical sense illuminates the relationship among knowledge, authority and power". For Anaru, these are commonly referred to as concepts of mātauranga, rangatiratanga, and mana. The messages from these parents, and young Sandra, took the meaning of pedagogy beyond a casual reference to teaching practices. Their messages took pedagogy to mean constructing relationships between learners and teachers where process matches product.

I would run the risk of trivialising a very complex area (of culturally responsive teaching) if I were to stop here. Compatibility with, and confidence in, established practices is important. Consequently, the leaders at Ngongotahā School were mindful that there needed to be individual construction of knowledge, as well as a social construction of knowledge. This involved assessing how individual students could work within the norms of the curriculum and its associated assessment systems. It is to that kaupapa that we now turn.

CHAPTER SIX

Messages from the assessments

As with any initiative of this kind, the specific student learning outcomes and achievements demonstrate the programme's effectiveness. Testing was carried out at regular intervals to monitor student learning and achievement. These data were included in the mid-year and end-of-year progress reports and presented to the Ngāti-Whakaue Education Endowment Trust Board, and to the Ngongotahā Primary School Board of Trustees. The Ngāti-Whakaue Enrichment Class assessment programme was administering a range of acknowledged standardised tests that specifically focused on the important facets of literacy and numeracy.

The first of these, the School Entry Assessment (Ministry of Education, 1997b), consists of three assessment tasks. The first, Concepts About Print (Clay, 1993) assesses emergent literacy. The second, Checkout/Rapua (Young-Loveridge, 1994) is a supermarket game to assess numeracy. The third, Tell Me/Ki Mai (McNaughton, 1995), is a storytelling activity assessing oral use of language. The results of these assessments alerted Gaye Ruru to the fact that there was a small but clearly defined group of students whose needs would be better served in the Enrichment Class.

At the time of student entry into the Ngāti-Whakaue Enrichment Class the Observational Survey (Six Year Net) (Clay, 1993), and a school-devised numeracy test (Ruru, 1998) were administered. This data provided a yardstick against which to measure specific learning gains for each individual student, and also helped with the shaping and modification of students' Individual Education Plans.

The academic results achieved by the students, both individually and collectively, showed considerable gains. Tables 6.1 to 6.8 below outline the learning achievements of the 12 students in the Ngāti-Whakaue Enrichment Class who were observed for the purposes of this study. Student No.10 and student No.11 left Ngongotahā School prior to the second assessment being carried out. Student No.12 returned to the Enrichment Class later that year. Ngongotahā School had adroit systems in place for monitoring attendance and mobility, fully recognising the unsettling effect of transience on young children. Brief analyses of the data associated with each test follow each table.

Table 6.1

Progress through successive reading levels (range 0 – 22)

		Reading Level (Clay, 1993)		
Student	D.O.B	February 2000	June 2000	Progress
1	11/93	2	2	0
2	07/93	4	16	12
3	02/94	4	16	12
4	06/93	4	13	9
5	04/94	2	5	3
6	11/93	2	2	0
7	06/93	5	16	11
8	12/93	1	3	2
9	06/93	0	3	3
10	10/93	0	2	2
11	09/93	3	Left	
12	10/93	4	Left	

Table 6.1 shows the gains were made in reading levels, over a two-term period, for all 10 students. The test places students on levels between 0 and 22, with 0 depicting pre-reading and 22 depicting a reading age of 7.5 to 8 years (or gold on the colour wheel). These results are based on the levelling used in the Ready to Read series made available to all schools in New Zealand by Learning Media (Ministry of Education, 1997a); this is regarded as a good instrument for ranking or grouping children during the first year of instruction, and for low progress readers in the second year (Clay, 1985). Because the students in this study were low progress readers in their second year, both Gaye Ruru and Bev

Anaru expressed a preference for this assessment tool. Of the 10 students who were able to be retested, four made considerable progress, four made moderate progress, and two stayed at the same level.

Table 6.2

BURT standardised word recognition test scores

BURT Standardised Word Recognition Test (Gilmore, Croft, and Reid, 1981)				
Student	D.O.B	February 2000	June 2000	Progress
1	11/93	3	8	5
2	07/93	5	27	22
3	02/94	12	25	13
4	06/93	3	25	22
5	04/94	17	32	15
6	11/93	2	12	10
7	06/93	8	26	18
8	12/93	0	3	3
9	06/93	0	12	12
10	10/93	6	11	5
11	09/93	6	Left	
12	10/93	10	Left	

Table 6.2 gives an indication of progress and achievement in word recognition over the same period. The BURT word recognition test describes children's level of attainment as a range rather than a reading age (allowing for the variations that occur in testing, which create measurement error). A score of 20 indicates an equivalent range of 5.10 to 6.04 for word recognition. Of the 10 students who were able to be retested, three made considerable progress, four made sound progress, and three showed moderate improvement in their word recognition levels. The three students who made considerable progress scored within range of their chronological age. None of the 10 students retested failed to make any progress at all.

The dictation test, Table 6.3, is used to determine the ability of students to record appropriate sounds in writing of oral dictation. In this test, there is a possible score of 37. This observation task directs the attention of teachers and children to phonemic awareness, a current emphasis in the research literature (Clay, 1993). According to Ruru and Anaru, this test forms part of the 6-Year

Table 6.3

Progress in ability to record appropriate sounds in writing of orally dictated sentences

		Dictation (Clay, 1993)		
Student	D.O.B	February 2000	June 2000	Progress
1	11/93	11	12	1
2	07/93	22	34	12
3	02/94	32	35	3
4	06/93	24	34	10
5	04/94	0	30	30
6	11/93	15	27	12
7	06/93	26	35	9
8	12/93	4	16	12
9	06/93	4	29	25
10	10/93	20	25	5
11	09/93	20	Left	
12	10/93	32	Left	

Observation Survey used by Ngongotahā Primary School. The data indicate that two students made considerable progress, five made sound progress, and three progressed moderately.

The letter identification test, Table 6.4, assesses recognition of upper and lower case letters by alphabet name, sound, or word. Children should score 54/54 by 6 years of age, if not earlier. For this test, it is more appropriate to analyse the data in terms of achieving a possible score of 54, rather than solely measuring the progress made. The data indicate that at the time of the initial test, three students knew fewer than half of the letter bank, and the other nine had a reasonable grasp of letter identification. Data from the second test shows that most students had managed to reach a level which would cause little or no concern to the teachers in the Ngāti-Whakaue Enrichment Class, in terms of ability to distinguish letters from one another.

The child hears and enjoys a story read by the teacher, who asks the child questions about features of print during the reading. Table 6.5 shows that six of the 10 students were achieving at a level compatible with their chronological age. The other four students scored slightly below their respective chronological

Table 6.4

Progress in ability to recognise upper and lower case letters by alphabet name, sound or word

		Letter Identification (Clay, 1993)		
Student	D.O.B	February 2000	June 2000	Progress
1	11/93	40	53	13
2	07/93	53	54	1
3	02/94	19	53	34
4	06/93	45	51	6
5	04/94	25	53	28
6	11/93	43	49	6
7	06/93	42	54	12
8	12/93	31	42	11
9	06/93	10	45	35
10	10/93	50	50	0
11	09/93	46	Left	
12	10/93	53	Left	

Table 6.5

Progress in ability to understand print concepts

		Concepts About Print (Clay, 1993)		
Student	D.O.B	February 2000	June 2000	Progress
1	11/93	12	16	4
2	07/93	15	19	4
3	02/94	11	20	9
4	06/93	12	15	3
5	04/94	9	20	11
6	11/93	9	13	4
7	06/93	18	21	3
8	12/93	11	13	2
9	06/93	10	11	1
10	10/93	8	12	4
11	09/93	9	Left	
12	10/93	16	Left	

ages, but made moderate progress. Student No.5 made considerable progress, moving up 11 levels. Again, progress was made by the 10 students who were retested.

Clay (1993) explains that a teacher can do an assessment of written vocabulary in any place at any time, needing nothing but their personal knowledge of how to make observations about children's writing behaviour. Such observations include the quality of letter formation, the number of letter forms the child uses, and the stock of words that the child can draw from. Teachers can also gain information about children's visual discrimination of print, and the left-to-right sequencing behaviour required to read.

There are marked individual differences among children in their first year of school, according to Clay. Table 6.6 shows that at the time of administering the first test, there were marked differences in written vocabulary among the students in the Ngāti-Whakaue Enrichment Class. However, satisfactory gains were made by all except one student.

Results for student No.10 showed losses, not gains. This result does not match the results achieved by this student across the other tests. Further analysis of the Written Vocabulary test may reveal some of the common variables known to apply to this type of assessment from time to time. These variables may include the state of the student's emotional, social, physical, and cognitive well-being at the time (Durie, 1994). While any number of assumptions may be made with regard to this result, Bev Anaru considered that the performances by student No.10 in other assessment tasks ruled out any cause for major concern. Bev's immediate concern was to awhi (monitor) the student's progress in written vocabulary in the context of the classroom dynamics.

Gaye Ruru described the maths assessment instrument used as a school-devised test, based on the number strand as outlined in the New Zealand Curriculum Framework (Ministry of Education, 1993). This test assesses numeracy knowledge, understanding, processing, and visual recognition of numerals. Students should be able to achieve a possible 60/60 at the end of Year 3. The nine students available for the initial test and the retest all showed improvement, ranging from 3 to 14. In relative terms, five students showed considerable improvement, two students made sound progress, and two students made moderate progress. Given that a 60/60 score would be expected of students at the end of Year 3, these data indicate that a reasonable number of these Year 2 students had the potential to meet this benchmark. Clearly, given the profound learning needs of some of these students, the expectation

Table 6.6

Progress in number of words written independently in 10 minutes

Written Vocabulary Test (Clay, 1993)

Student	D.O.B	February 2000	June 2000	Progress
1	11/93	8	15	7
2	07/93	9	25	16
3	02/94	0	25	25
4	06/93	9	21	12
5	04/94	0	25	25
6	11/93	3	18	15
7	06/93	21	28	7
8	12/93	2	5	3
9	06/93	2	13	11
10	10/93	26	19	-7
11	09/93	14	Left	
12	10/93	37	Left	

Table 6.7

Numeracy knowledge, understanding, processing and visual recognition of numerals

Maths (Ruru, 1998)

Student	D.O.B	February 2000	June 2000	Progress
1	11/93	13	26	13
2	07/93	31	39	7
3	02/94	28	41	13
4	06/93	21	30	9
5	04/94	Absent	Absent	Hospital with pneumonia
6	11/93	15	26	11
7	06/93	29	43	14
8	12/93	10	14	4
9	06/93	15	18	3
10	10/93	11	22	11
11	09/93	11	Left	
12	10/93	24	Left	

that every one of them would attain the 60/60 score appears unreasonable. Student No.8 and student No.9 were identified as having high, complex, and continuing needs and were being considered for Ongoing and Renewable Resourcing Scheme (ORRS) support. Gaye Ruru was adamant that by working on their self-esteem, these students would experience success in any case – but in a social rather than academic domain.

The individual results of most of the Ngāti-Whakaue Enrichment Class students shown here reinforced the effectiveness of both the programme content and the programme delivery. Further analyses of these data highlight the overall success of the unit and the progress made in wider terms. After four months in the Ngāti-Whakaue Enrichment Class:

- Sixty percent of the Year 2 students achieved oral language gains of more than one year, with the average being 12 months, and the range being 0 to 1 year 7 months.
- The average instructional reading improvement was 5.4 Reading Recovery levels, with the range being 0 to 12 levels.
- The average improvement for Letter Identification was 14 letters/sounds, with the range being 0 to 35.
- The average gain for written vocabulary was 12 words, with the range being from –7 to 25 words.
- The average score on the BURT word recognition test was 18 words, with the range being 3 to 32 words.

This overall progress was achieved with students whose entry data started as low as 3 years 6 months in Assessment of Oral Language, and a score of zero on 50 percent of all tests, after being at school for approximately 10 to 20 months. The students in this cohort had been in the unit for either one or two terms.

The standardised tests were only one aspect of assessment. The Ngāti-Whakaue Enrichment Class teachers looked at the global evaluation results and the implications of performance. Assessment was concerned with qualitative as well as quantitative components of performance on related tasks, observed both formally and informally, within and outside the learning setting. Although testing, unfortunately, can become an end in itself in schools (Wallace, Larsen, and Elksnin, 1992), according to Smith, Polloway, Patton, and Dowdy (1998, p. 65) it "seeks to capture a more complete picture of the student through the determination of current functioning levels. Forming this picture is essential to effective educational planning and instruction." Armed with a range of data,

Bev Anaru considered that she was better positioned to prepare the students in her class to "taste success".

Anaru acknowledged that it was easy for children in this group to develop a sense of failure – a picture of themselves as someone who was "dumb" and "no good". She refused, however, to acknowledge any deficits as residing in these children themselves. She aimed to help them develop self-respect, and respect for others and for the environment. From this starting point, Anaru believed they would develop confidence and a work ethic. She was adamant that children must have approval from adults (parents, teachers), as well as those of their own age, if they are to develop successfully. Moreover, Anaru was aware of the pervasive influence of their Māoritanga on their well-being, learning, and social development. Because the children in this classroom were Māori, the manifestation of their values and culture would need to have real presence in the classroom. She held that this would be evidenced in the way they worked (work styles), thought (worldview), and reacted to the classroom structure, activities, interactions, and discipline.

Compared with the volumes of literature on learning enhancement and behaviour modification, only a few studies to date have systematically examined the relationship between ethnic identity and school performance. This study found a positive relationship between ethnic identity (a sense of belonging in their Māoritanga), through the teacher's ability to stress pride and commitment to the cultural background of all children in the classroom, and school performance. The study also examined the verbal and non-verbal communication processes between teacher and students in the classroom. It specifically focused on the direct and indirect messages that Bev Anaru communicated to the students, both consciously and subconsciously. Anaru's professional integrity, and the influences this had on students' learning processes, were explored by employing a range of methods. These included: observation of classroom activities and procedures; focused interviews in groups, and individually with key stakeholders; samples of children's work, and analyses of children's progress; and consideration of how successful the programme had been in meeting the outcomes that the project had set out to achieve. What emerged were fine examples of culturally relevant teaching – the kind of teaching that uses the students' culture to help them to achieve success (Ladson-Billings, 1990).

CHAPTER SEVEN

Messages for teachers

Manuka Henare (1999) alerts educators to the need to hold on to the cultural roots. He refers to the words of the first Māori woman ever to graduate with a degree through the New Zealand university system, Dame Mira Szaszy. Speaking to the 1993 Māori graduands' capping ceremony at Victoria University of Wellington, Dame Mira offered an ethical response to today's world, claiming that the essence of being Māori can be found in ancestral values:

> ... what we need in essence is a new Māori humanism, that is, a humanism based on ancient values but versed in contemporary idiom. Our current humanism does not seem to have found its balance – with the rich lurching forward, disposing of their cultural roots and becoming rootless, and the poor, particularly unemployed, becoming poorer without even the sustenance of cultural or spiritual strengths (Szaszy, 1993, p. 7).

The educational programme provided at Ngongotahā School's Enrichment Class embodied examples of a humanism that embraced ancient values in modern times. Rather than "lurching forward", the programme was seen to be "reaching out", particularly to tamariki with special educational needs. It was also seen to be reaching back to access the cultural sustenance from tipuna, finding that balance that Dame Mira had prescribed.

The Ngāti-Whakaue Enrichment Class involved the establishment of a working relationship among three groups – a special class within a mainstream school, its community, and a tribal trust board – for mutual benefit. As a consequence, the paradox of inclusion, versus the need for separate space within which the indigenous culture can thrive, emerges. The Ngāti-Whakaue programme clearly understood that culture was central to learning. The programme saw culture as shaping the thinking processes of the students, as well as defining the modes of communication, and receiving and giving information. The discussions and commentaries from significant individuals and groups, who had developed a sound knowledge of the site leaders' respective pedagogic approaches, acknowledged the quintessence of Māoritanga.

Significant agreement can be found among most educators, researchers, and parents committed to the appropriate education of students with learning and behaviour difficulties, regardless of their views of current reform. Nearly all the advocates for these students want effective education in the least restrictive environment. According to Kauffman (1993), such an environment accommodates students with special problems, dismisses stigmatisation, promotes parental participation in decision-making, and collaborates with service providers. Despite this, many of special education's problems will persist, whether the current calls for full inclusion are answered or ignored. Kauffman is concerned that too many students are poorly served by special education, because their programmes are not really special – that is, they are no more appropriate than the programmes they would receive in general education. Conversely, one might also argue that too many students are poorly served by regular education, primarily because the learner-teacher interactions, which are the core of effective instruction and culturally responsive pedagogy, are inadequate.

Inclusion may carry a danger of marginalising cultural differences, through trying to minimise the nuances, values, and beliefs of indigenous students. The information provided by teachers, parents, and indeed the students themselves of the Ngāti-Whakaue Enrichment Class implied that mainstream education may not be capable of providing an appropriate education to all students, and may even be harmful to some (Māori) students with learning and behaviour difficulties.

An inclusive school is seen as one that educates all students in the mainstream. It also means providing all students within the mainstream with appropriate educational programmes that are challenging and geared to their capabilities and needs. An inclusive school is a place where everyone belongs, is accepted, and both supports and is supported by his or her peers and other members of the community, in the course of having his or her educational needs met (Stainback and Stainback, 1990). As enthusiastic as we might be about this approach, some schools may not be able to do this. Mainstream may not be providing an appropriate education to all students. What if retention (in mainstream) of students with severe learning and behaviour difficulties actually closes the door on many Māori students' ability to learn to their potential, and improve their behaviour?

Until all schools can facilitate appropriate education programmes and support for "every" student in mainstream, programmes such as Ngongotahā's Ngāti-Whakaue Enrichment Class must be given space – the kind of space which is culturally, as well as academically and socially, responsive. Fuchs and Fuchs (1995) contend that when students are not benefiting from instruction in a mainstream setting, a compromise must be struck between legitimate social (including cultural) needs, and equally valid instructional needs. Two appropriate solutions emerge:

- Classroom teachers and resource teachers need to find generic teaching strategies that work for all students.
- These strategies should be introduced in cultural contexts, and with culturally appropriate pedagogies, that still represent and affirm the language and culture of Māori students.

This is not a plea to provide more schools or classrooms similar to the Ngāti-Whakaue Enrichment Class. Rather it is a plea to educational administrators, consultants, and classroom teachers to take notice of the principles and practices that underpinned the Ngāti-Whakaue programme, and encourage the introduction of these principles and practices, where necessary, into regular classrooms.

The Ngāti-Whakaue Enrichment Class was a convincing example of using culturally appropriate teaching to improve the academic and social performance of underachieving Māori students. The programme showed that Māori students will perform better, on multiple measures of achievement, when teaching is filtered through their own cultural experiences and frames of reference. The programme gave a strong message to classroom teachers and special education consultants that there are key components of culturally responsive teaching which they must take on board, given that they are the carriers of these messages to and in regular classrooms. The key components of culturally responsive teaching include teacher caring, teacher attitudes and expectations, formal and informal bicultural curriculum, culturally informed classroom discourse, and cultural congruity in teaching and learning strategies (Gay, 2000). The Ngāti-Whakaue Enrichment Class programme provided evidence of these key components.

Gay (2000) asserts that culturally responsive teaching realises the importance not only of academic achievement, but also of maintaining cultural identity and heritage. As in other studies on culturally relevant teaching (Ladson-Billings, 1994; Lipman, 1995; Macfarlane, 1997), the Ngāti-Whakaue Enrichment Class programme demonstrated that when students were part of a more collective effort designed to encourage academic and social excellence, expectations were clearly expressed, skills were taught, and interpersonal relationships were exhibited. Students were held accountable to the larger group. In addition, they behaved like members of an extended family (whānau) – assisting and supporting each other. A strong presence of these concepts and approaches was identified and interpreted in the Ngāti-Whakaue Enrichment Class. That this programme was not located in a mainstream setting should not be a major concern. The critical issue must be that the pedagogies could be useful in making regular classrooms more inclusive.

One of the realities of the field of education is that researchers and practitioners are often working from different and sometimes competing paradigms. Instead of asking questions about the pros and cons of mainstreaming or alternatives to mainstreaming, we should be asking ourselves what we need to do to make inclusion even better. It is argued that in New Zealand schools, inclusion can be made even better by drawing from the examples of multidimensional, culturally responsive pedagogies that enable students to achieve a sense of pride in their culture, and at the same time to experience success in their learning. The Ngāti-Whakaue Enrichment Class programme provided such an example of culturally appropriate teaching and learning. The programme was inclusive in ways that many regular classrooms may not be inclusive, in that it continually affirmed the language and culture of Māori students. However, more sites like the Ngāti-Whakaue Enrichment Class are not the solution. The solution is to encourage regular classroom teachers to adopt similar practices when working with Māori students.

CHAPTER EIGHT

Strategies for teachers

Motivation, personality, behaviour, and attitude are just some of the categories which underpin theoretical and practical work in modern psychology. Each of these concepts has assumed their contemporary meanings in curricula and classroom management, and each has persuasive explanations for the directions of human actions. The rapid development towards a knowledge-based economy and society has presented existing education systems with serious challenges, as well as great opportunities. Yibing (2000) contends that fundamental reforms and innovations in education policies, structures, and functions are required to meet these challenges, as the learning society makes relentless technological progress. However, mapping the cultural terrain of education into the inaugural decade of this new millennium should explore a knowledge framework which continues to foster indigenous worldviews. This chapter considers some of the values and concepts, abilities and skills of Māori people, accumulated through many years of experience, learning, development, and transmission.

Harris (1996), in discussing the processes of collaboration within a multicultural society, emphasises that developing cultural competence is important for teachers and educational consultants working in inclusive education. Harris makes a number of suggestions: understanding one's own cultural perspective in relation to the perspectives of culturally diverse learners; using effective interpersonal communications strategies within a cultural context; understanding the roles assumed by teachers working with students who are culturally and linguistically diverse; and promoting the use of culturally fair and appropriate assessment and instructional strategies. In

New Zealand schools, both classroom teachers and resource teachers have a long way to go towards understanding and responding to the major differences between Māori and non-Māori students. Developing effective learning and teaching strategies for Māori students, and for students of other minority cultural groups, requires classroom teachers and resource teachers to learn to think, explain, and act according to predominant metaphors and theories of diverse cultures, and not simply in terms of the metaphors and theories of their own (majority) culture (Glynn, 1998).

According to Wolfendale (1992), all initiatives in education can be located in their uniquely apposite time and place. In other words, there is a context, if not an explanation, for the origins and justifications of practices identified as new, different, and innovative. A confluence of knowledge and basic skills seems to have been transmitted across generations of educational theorists, analysts, and practitioners. An historical analysis reveals the enduring nature of a number of core concepts and activities, even if their frequency and function change over time.

Barlow (1993) considers that while some of the Māori concepts may not have great relevance to today's society, others are the core for understanding Māori culture as it is practised today, and are also concepts which are likely to be relevant in the future. Ritchie (1992) contends that since Māori people insist on wholeness, it is hard to portray Māori concepts and values in analytical form. In this section I will describe, in turn, five Māori concepts, in terms of understanding a Māori worldview. These are whanaungatanga, rangatiratanga, manaakitanga, kotahitanga, and pumanawatanga. I will then attempt to articulate these concepts as the key cultural concept bases for effective classroom management strategies. It should be noted that these concepts do not exist in isolation from each other – more often than not, they co-exist or are amalgamated. Since Māori insist on wholeness, this is quite natural.

Cultural concept one: whanaungatanga

Whanaungatanga is described by Bishop (1996) as the process of establishing relationships in a Māori context. Graham Smith (1995) acknowledges that whānau (and to an extent whanaungatanga) has multiple meanings, but in recent times is often defined as the notion of a group sharing an association, based on things such as kinship, common locality, and common interests. For Ritchie (1992), whanaungatanga is the basic element that holds things Māori together; it affirms and transcends tribal identity and everything comes back to kinship. Essentially, it is about the heart of relationships.

The message is clear: relationships in the classroom and among the school community must be established and maintained. Interviews with Māori secondary students (Bishop et al., 2002; Macfarlane, 1995) who sometimes presented challenges for staff revealed that they wanted their teachers to discuss what their lives were like outside school, and they wanted to be more engaged in classroom activities and school systems. Developing an understanding of students' lives also enables the teacher to increase the relevance of lessons, and make examples more meaningful.

Consider this: Organise a class hui whakataki (initial gathering)

Begin the year with a class (or syndicate) hui – not a powhiri, but with elements similar to a powhiri. Involve local kaumātua (senior men and women from the local iwi) in an authentic way. Authenticity is achieved by involving the kaumātua in the planning, acknowledging their mana by seeking their advice and following it, ensuring that their voices are heard, and allowing space for their leadership qualities to be expressed. This approach is in contrast to the one of "dial a kaumātua" where they are merely "ring ins" – their services are used and they are then dispatched forthwith. It is not uncommon these days to offer kaumātua a koha for their services. All families and whānau should be invited to the hui whakataki regardless of their ethnicity, thus giving credence to the inclusive ritual that it is. The hui can be intricate or simple; the context will determine the level of intensity that it takes. However, most hui like this involve whaikōrero (speech-making), waiata (song), karakia (prayer), and hongi (salutation). Before this hui takes place, the class should undertake a unit of study on hui, so that they have an adequate understanding of the parts that make up the whole. One teaching point, for example, would be that the hongi is a sign of peace and well-being. Students can be encouraged to analyse these Māori practices and discuss the potential of the principles (not necessarily the practices) for application in an emotionally healthy classroom. Kai (partaking of food) is also a necessary part of the hui.

Because such a unit of study would have a strong Māori orientation, it lends itself to several Māori-preferred learning styles, in particular to ako and rote learning. Metge (1983) refers to ako as the unified co-operation of learner and teacher in a single enterprise. According to Glynn and Bishop (1995), ako is manifested by blending the distinction between teacher and learner, and between teaching and learning. In this context, an example of ako would be encouraging Māori students who have a level of competence in their culture to take on the role of teaching their peers, and possibly their teachers. The hui whakataki ritual would require that all students learn a waiata. Discussions about the origins and meanings of the waiata would precede the learning of the words and the tune. The latter is likely to involve rote learning, a technique valued by Māori as an effective means of taking the learning to mastery level. Glynn (1998) notes that rote learning strategies should not be associated with trivial or surface learning, but with learning that is both complex and deep.

The hui whakataki is but one form of Māori hui. There are many others that classrooms and schools can use, such as formal classroom discussions, students' birthdays, class or school social events, or preparation for a classroom visit to a marae. It is in the context of hui like this that Māoritanga is most deeply expressed. Salmond (1975, p. 2) reminds us that "throughout the hui Māori is the ceremonial language, Māori people dominate, Māori food is eaten, and Māori rituals are practised".

Consider this: Know your students' backgrounds

Although the specific causes of misunderstandings occurring in schools differ, depending upon the context, there is one common element – polarised communication. Gudykunst (1994) contends that polarised communication exists when groups or individuals look out for their own interests, and have little or no concern for the interests of others. Many teachers express these small intolerances in their conversations with their colleagues and students, without being aware of doing so. Lack of interest in the backgrounds of others will stultify communication and harm the whanaungatanga process.

Teachers, both Māori and non-Māori, need to gather information about the iwi and hapū that are tangata-whenua in the school's locality. They need to read about it, talk to local people about it, digest it, and, when ready, experience the parts of it which they are comfortable with. I had to do these things when my work took me from my own tribal area of Te Arawa to the Waikato tribal area. While I had some background knowledge of the Tainui waka and its iwi, it was not considerable. Given that I was to be working in a university bearing the Waikato name, it was in my interests to familiarise myself with some of the history, icons, and people. Reading about and talking to others about the kingitanga, poukai, Princess Te Puea, raupatu, the river of bends and esoteric minders (Waikato taniwharau, he piko he taniwha), and observing and participating in hui at Waikato University's Te Kōhinga Marama marae proved both helpful and useful. These activities made me more insightful about and more understanding of the tribe's trials, tribulations, bravado, and successes. Carrying out these tasks was neither strenuous nor time consuming. I will never be one of them; that cannot be. However, by knowing more about the tangata-whenua, I felt more at ease and comfortable within and among them. It is no different for teachers. Build relationships by knowing your students' backgrounds, as well as the backgrounds of the local Māori iwi.

Another example of this was my experiences co-ordinating and teaching Māori-bicultural courses for the Resource Teachers Learning and Behaviour (RTLB) university training programme. One of the assignments in Course One (which occurs in the first of four semesters over two years) required RTLB to gather and reflect on information toward presenting a report about one school in which they had worked. The report had to include information on: the iwi holding mana whenua status; the different iwi represented among Māori students in a selected classroom; the proportion of Māori students and staff; a description of resources for Māori students; an assessment of the respect for mana Māori in the school; and a pūrākau (story or legend) relating to the district. RTLB were also required to compare and contrast their findings with those of other colleagues, and report on the extent to which mana Māori was respected across several schools. My suspicions were that setting such an assignment did not do anything for my popularity rating. Perhaps some RTLB thought things such as "What's the point?" or "What has this got to do with learning and behaviour?" The point is whanaungatanga – depolarising communication by respectfully knowing more about other people and other ways of doing things. Whanaungatanga is the strategy that can help teachers and resource teachers to be more effective when working with Māori students and whānau.

Let us return to the RTLB assignment. The course co-ordinators, nationally, were impressed with the quality of the 700 assignments returned. There was evidence of careful and respectful consultation with kaumātua and Māori staff in their schools. There was evidence that kaumātua and Māori staff had been willing to share some beautiful pūrākau (traditional legends) relating to mountains, rivers, and tribal ancestors in the respective regions, including some reference to both pre-contact and post-contact events. RTLB obtained some telling comparative information on the proportions of Māori students and staff in their local schools. They identified examples of careful collaboration between schools and their Māori communities over delivery of Te Reo Māori programmes. However, they also identified examples where the language and cultural aspirations of strong and vibrant Māori communities had yet to be addressed in their local schools (Macfarlane and Glynn, 2001).

In endeavouring to assess the extent to which mana Māori was evident in schools, RTLB consulted with kaumātua, Māori teachers, and Māori support staff, and ensured that these voices and positions were reflected in their assignments. RTLB were able to identify ways in which they could improve their own work in helping schools to meet the learning and behavioural needs of their Māori students. Most importantly, they learned the lesson that "culture counts" when it comes to devising effective ways to improve learning and behavioural outcomes for Māori students.

The reason for citing this example is not a call for all classroom teachers to do something similar, although that may seem a desirable option. The reason is to offer teachers ideas of how whanaungatanga can bring about professional growth. Many classroom teachers I know plan units of study for their children based on whakapapa and local history, which are not altogether dissimilar to the RTLB university assignment. Such is the ubiquitous nature of education that content and approach can be adapted according to the context.

Consider this: People in the community are excellent resources

Some of the best educational resources are the people in the community. In the school communities across the country, local experts in Māoritanga abound. Most of these people willingly give of their time to share their skills in the arts, crafts, and humanities. My own experience as head teacher of a school for secondary students experiencing emotional and behavioural difficulties involved Māori leaders and experts as role models and teachers. One example was when Mita Mohi came to the school to talk to my students about mana Māori, about being proud of who they are. Mita, one of Māoridom's most accomplished exponents of the taiaha, went on to take the boys through a wānanga (learning course) on the practical and spiritual elements of mau-taiaha. Their interest level was high, their attention to detail meticulous, and their enthusiasm to attain mastery overwhelming. I could not do what Mita had done, because he had the mana and the knowledge in this discipline that evolved from years of experience and scholarship in the traditional arts and humanities. There are also many younger Māori role models from iwi who often offer to visit schools and to work with students. Take, for instance, the Morrison cousins. Imagine what Temuera's glamour or Scotty's sagacity would do for the motivation of young Māori in our schools!

Consider this: Involve parents and families

Parents and students need to be involved in discussions affecting them. They should not have things done for them without their full consultation and participation in decision-making (Gadd, 1976). Parental participation is an indispensable ingredient in academic excellence. Winzer and Mazurek (1998) assert that the closer the parent moves towards the education of his or her child, the more the potential impact on the child for educational achievement. This achievement is multiple; it relates to academic progress, fewer discipline problems, increased self-esteem and social skills, better attendance, and improved attitude.

There are no hard and fast rules for involving Māori parents in their child's or children's schooling. The way that Māori parents react to and interact with the school differs. The following suggestions are helpful when interacting with Māori parents:
- Find out about the families' backgrounds, their marae, their children.
- Visit the home, but a positive phone call should precede the visit. Don't break upsetting news over the phone.
- Check whether parents feel comfortable with your ideas, actions, or intentions.
- If you lack a little confidence in their culture, be up front. Tell parents about your unfamiliarity and that you may make mistakes.
- Be personable and warm, and indirect. Many Māori parents do not like confrontation.
- Initial contact with parents should be just that, initial contact. So be firm, be brief, be gone. Kia manawanui, kia poto, me haere (this is also a good classroom discipline strategy).

There are many recommended practices teachers can use to connect more effectively with parents. Those listed above are starting points to reduce the alienation that some Māori parents frequently experience. Parents of students experiencing learning and behaviour difficulties also have aspirations for their futures. As educators, it is important that we do not kill these dreams.

Consider this: Co-operative learning works

Co-operative learning is an excellent example of how whanaungatanga can be manifested in the classroom. Co-operative learning is "a generic term for the instructional organisation of children into mixed ability study groups in which participants cooperate with one another to achieve academic goals" (Rich, cited in Winzer and Mazurek, 1998, p. 302). Within these groups, the reaching of goals is possible only by way of the total participation of peers in the activities.

Brown and Thomson (2000) declare that co-operative learning contexts are able to enhance both academic and social skills by providing structures that allow effective learning strategies to develop. Further, Brown and Thomson query how essential social skills are able to be learned well without a co-operative group structure. Medcalf (1995) outlines the two key components of co-operative learning essential for achievement gains: firstly, group rewards are contingent on all members reaching either individual or collective goals; secondly, individual accountability to the group is necessary. These components provide incentives for students to work together and communicate effectively. Because co-operative learning combines academic and social skills, the symbiotic nature of co-operative learning is able to be further highlighted. The process that ensures enhanced learning results from, and is reliant on, social skills and respectful interactions. These in turn are enhanced because of greater academic gains (Bateman, 2003).

Ongoing research into classroom practice clearly indicates that co-operative learning is advantageous for all students, not just those with special learning and teaching needs (Brown and Thomson, 2000; Fuchs and Fuchs, 1994; Good and Brophy, 1994; Johnson, Johnson, and Maruyama, 1983). It is also clear that co-operative learning contexts are advantageous to Māori students, because they include the social concept of ako, which recognises the concurrent and reciprocal nature of teaching and learning (Macfarlane and Glynn, cited in Brown and Thomson, 2000). Tuakana status (the status of senior students) and kaiarahitanga (leadership) qualities are shown in co-operative learning by what Metge (1983) refers to as "modelling" or "learning through exposure" and "learning in groups". Kapahaka is also a form of co-operative learning. In the kapahaka learning paradigm, new members are placed among more experienced members until they too obtain mastery. Moreover, contributing to group process is as important as achieving the group goals. Co-operative learning in the classroom, however, is also a way of bringing about cross-ethnic socialisation. Johnson, Johnson, and Maruyama (1983), contend that when children from diverse backgrounds work co-operatively together, the status of group members tends to be equalised, with all members developing personal regard and respect for one another.

Bear in mind that co-operative learning is a structured process, sometimes intricate in nature. Therefore, in the first instance, co-operative skills have to be taught. Subsequently, details such as room arrangement, student placement, and evaluation of learning performance have to be seriously considered. Further modification of one or two strategies may be necessary for the involvement of Māori students. For example, "face-to-face" active interaction may have the potential to present itself as too "in-your-face" active interaction. Perhaps Māori students would be more responsive to a "kanohi ki te kanohi" approach to this strategy. Graham (2003) describes "kanohi ki te kanohi" as a trusting and sharing approach, wherein each other's credibility is nurtured. Explanations surrounding this Māori perception of connecting would be fitting, as it would present co-operative learning as non-threatening in its structure. Māori students, in the main, have a co-operative orientation towards learning and life, and the whanaungatanga aspects within co-operative learning classroom structures have the potential to facilitate improved academic engagement.

Cultural concept two: rangatiratanga

Holding and exercising status within an event or community is a central meaning of the concept of rangatiratanga. Applicable to both males and females, rangatiratanga, according to Ritchie (1992), "is related to effectiveness, to being good at things or getting things done . . . it may refer to drawing an additional boost of power, of strength, of mana" (p. 70). That rangatiratanga is linked to the concept of mana there is little doubt. Barlow (1993) explains that in modern times, the term mana has taken on various meanings, including the power of gods, ancestors, land, and individuals (mana atua, mana tipuna, mana whenua, mana tangata). For the purposes of education, mana tangata appears a most appropriate complementary factor to the concept of rangatiratanga. Barlow elaborates that mana tangata "is the power acquired by an individual according to his or her ability and effort to develop skills and gain knowledge in particular areas" (p. 62). It would be fair to say that evidence of rangatiratanga and mana tangata were portrayed in the Ngāti-Whakaue Enrichment Class, as they are by teachers in numerous other classrooms around the country. Essentially, rangatiratanga in the classroom is about good teaching that is culturally inclusive. The elements of good teaching apply to all settings, regardless of the students within these settings. Winzer and Mazurek (1998) maintain that implicitly or explicitly, every educator in every setting must have a particular range of skills and abilities. They add that teachers must know about the curriculum, the pedagogy, and the environment. This means that teachers must know what is to be taught, how it is to be taught, and where and when it should be taught.

Initiatives for reforming schools are occurring across the nation, as are Ministry of Education contracts for research into student achievement or non-achievement. These initiatives are focused on finding the causal factors (which we have known for years), and reporting on these. Good information and recommendations come about as a consequence of these initiatives, but they also need to motivate students.

The Ngāti-Whakaue Enrichment Class is an example of a pro-active initiative that is iwi endorsed and school driven. Another exciting initiative that is focused on rasing the motivation and achievement levels of Māori students is the Ministry of Education's Te Kotahitanga Project.

Using information gathered from students, whānau, principals, and teachers from four schools, the Te Kotahitanga research team put together an effective teaching profile, and developed a professional development programme around it (Bishop, Berryman, Richardson, and Tiakiwai, 2002). The Te Kotahitanga Project developed a profile of effective teaching; the Ngāti-Whakaue Enrichment Class appeared to have those elements in it. This does not mean that the Te Kotahitanga teaching profile or the "Bev Anaru factor" have all the answers. However, over many years of examining the influences on student learning, there is a general consensus about what makes a difference in the culturally inclusive classroom. Central to these considerations are two key elements – different in name but similar in meaning – these are "mana" and "withitness".

We have already seen, albeit briefly, how a number of scholars ascribe meanings to the concept of mana. Clearly, mana is a force that brings about change in such a way that it can move people (Tate, 1990). This is in tandem with what Jacob Kounin (1977) called "withitness". Kounin's work is cited in most writings about classroom management. He discusses the importance of momentum and smoothness in the classroom activities, and how group alerting and student accountability are critical. "Withitness" is the factor that most clearly differentiates between effective teachers and ineffective teachers.

Consider this: Scan the room

Many Māori orators and leaders have the knack of summing up the environment and knowing what is going on around them, even while they are in full flight. Those doing the observing or listening are convinced that the leader does in fact know what is occurring in front of them, to the side of them, and behind them! Teachers with mana and withitness have the ability to convince students of their awareness, and to communicate their awareness through words and actions. If a student is off task, it may be necessary for a teacher to make eye contact. If necessary, a brief statement may be in order: "E hika, me whakatika to waka" ("Hey there, bring your canoe back on line." In other words, get back on task). Bill Rogers (1997) recommends that a "thank you" at the end of a request denotes an expectation that the teacher's request will be carried out. Beginning the request by using the student's name tends to give the message more urgency – for example, "Piripi, pass that book back to Janine, thank you."

Consider this: Use effective body language

Expert performances in the haka, waiata, whaikōrero, and opera often allow the performers' body language to carry their messages and their moods. New Zealand's most renowned musicians, such as Sir Howard Morrison, can move from easy to intense, from light to deep, with their voice, lyrics, and body language, which in combination capture the mood. Dame Kiri Te Kanawa uses body language to the same effect in opera roles. Carlos Spencer does not have to tell anyone how enthusiastic he is about the game of rugby, and Winston Peters does not have to proclaim his passion for politics – their body language does a great deal of the talking for them. The artistry of teaching draws heavily on body language. Fredric Jones (1987) maintains that body language is excellent for revealing thoughts, feelings, and intentions. It can show that the teacher is calmly in control – and calmness conveys strength. The body language that Jones emphasises includes eye contact, physical proximity, body carriage, facial expression, and gestures. Māori perceive "te to o te tangata" to be concerned with how a person presents themselves in terms of humarietanga (gentleness), ngakautanga (genuineness, coming from the heart), and tika (respect for the context and process).

Consider this: Make eye contact

Mrs Te Aonui is taking the kapahaka group through its paces. In the back row, Pita and Richard are inattentive, and their behaviour is distracting others in the group. Mrs Te Aonui pauses and makes eye contact with the two boys. The short pause is enough to cause quiet among the group. The eye contact is enough to let the boys know that Mrs Te Aonui is not impressed with their behaviour, and they must go back to the task at hand. Mrs Te Aonui's eyes sweep the room. She can also make eye contact in an approving way towards Harata, whose keenness to master the task is acknowledged.

To "takahi the mana" of a person is to "trample on their dignity". This could quite easily have happened if Mrs Te Aonui had opted to bawl the boys out in front of their peers. Had Mrs Te Aonui done that, it would seem more than likely that her mana would have also been dealt a blow, as students may have seen her reaction as a sign of weakness, or narrow-mindedness, on her part. The relationship between students and teachers could be impaired by employing the wrong strategy, and it would take time to rebuild that relationship. This strategy employed by Mrs Te Aonui is a good example of "work smarter, not harder". Mrs Te Aonui also worked smarter with Harata. Some Māori students also experience whakamā (embarrassment) when they are praised openly. If we imagine that Harata is a shy child, then Mrs Te Aonui's eye contact and gentle nod of approval (no pause in this case, because behaviour redirection was not necessary) seems an effective choice.

Consider this: Use physical proximity

The inattentiveness displayed by Pita and Richard may also have been addressed by Mrs Te Aonui gaining proximity to the boys in the back row. This is often referred to as "working the crowd". Good teachers set up the context so that it is not difficult for them to get from one point to another quickly and unobtrusively. A classic example of this is the way that Eraia Kiel (the leader of the Manaia performing arts ensemble) is capable of gliding amongst this kapahaka group, even while the most stirring performance is in motion. Eraia's actions would be likely to reassure his party, through his physical presence. As a classroom management strategy, Jones (1987) advises teachers to remain calm, move near the hoha student, establish brief eye contact, and say nothing. The student will usually return immediately to proper behaviour.

Consider this: Use demeanour – body carriage, facial expression, gesture – te tō o te tangata

I recall vividly, and with great affection, my secondary schooling at Hato Petera College. It was, and still is, an environment where collegiality, camaraderie, and competition quite naturally and liberally coexist. I could call up numerous examples, but I will draw upon just one – the annual whaikōrero festival at Hato Petera, when the students participating demonstrated their unique oratory skills. One student won this event two years running. After all these years, I can still picture his victorious performances, probably because of his demeanour as much as the content of the speech. Whai's body carriage made him look in control, and his facial expressions communicated the mood he wished to express. While oratory skills are not a prime function of teachers (although tutelage may be useful for some), their demeanour can send out important messages to students. Jones contends that students quickly read the teacher's body language and are able to tell whether the teacher is in charge, tired, disinterested, or intimidated. Teachers whose body language signals lethargy have the potential to prompt students into behaving in an unacceptable way, simply because the teacher is not presenting with mana, or rangatiratanga. On the other hand, good posture and confident body carriage send out messages of enthusiasm and withitness, which is far more likely to get students interested and attending to the tasks in hand. Frowns or a very slight shake of the head show the teacher's disapproval and can address misbehaviour before it escalates. Flashing eyes and a deep breath can let the student know that limits are being extended. These expressions are often better than verbal tirades. Nods of approval and warm smiles, used in a timely and proportional way, are also effective incentives.

Consider this: Use assertiveness – ihi

In New Zealand, several intervention programmes that draw on traditional Māori principles and concepts have been developed in recent years. Ted Glynn and his colleagues' Hei Awhina Mātua programme has a strong whānau and community positioning (Glynn, Berryman, Atvars, and Harawira, 1997). The Cultural Self-Review (Bevan-Brown, 2003) provides guidelines for culturally inclusive practices for Māori learners. The Hikairo Rationale (Macfarlane, 1997), advances a bicultural approach for working with Māori students experiencing behaviour difficulties. While this latter approach has seven components to it, it is to the first two that I will refer, as they most strongly depict the concept of ihi, or assertiveness.

The Hikairo Rationale is so named because of the way peaceful resolution was reached following the Ngapuhi and Te Arawa encounters on Mokoia Island in 1823. According to Stafford (1967), the Ngāti-Rangiwewehi Chief, Hikairo, spoke and acted with such mana and influence that the illustrious chief Hongi Hika declared that calmness and powerfulness were not incompatible. On this occasion, Hikairo's assertive dialogue, fundamental assurances, and simple sincerity brought about a change of attitude and behaviour.

The Hikairo approach is appropriate for working with both Māori and non-Māori students and teachers, even though its guiding values and metaphors come from within a Māori worldview. The traditional Māori value of aroha (love) has a very real place in the model. Aroha does not depict a "soft" approach. In the context of discipline, aroha connotes co-operation, understanding, reciprocity, and warmth. The Hikairo programme has these qualities in abundance, and is simultaneously assertive.

The first step of the Hikairo approach is called "Huakina Mai", meaning to open doorways. This step proposes that from the outset, it is crucial that the teacher gets to know the students and that the students get to know the teacher's expectations. For those students who display high levels of disruptive behaviour, the opening of doorways must occur in the very early stages. Part of the Huakina Mai process involves establishing rules. Rules are expectations of how whānau members are expected to behave towards each other. Rules are put in place to protect the rights of the whole group. From day one, the teacher is encouraged to enter into a contract of "fairness" with the students. This can be expressed in its most simple form by the teacher saying, "I promise you that as long as you are at this school, I will always be fair to you. Always. All I want in return is that you are fair to me. Do we have an understanding?" This draws on two key principles for changing behaviour: "model what you want" and "get in early" (Glynn et al., 1997).

A clear understanding of the protocol of the whānau aspect of the classroom should be discussed with each student in the very early stages, and then revisited from time to time as the need arises. Pastoral time before classes start in the morning is a crucial dimension of Huakina Mai. During this time, the teacher can allow the students to share their most recent experiences and gauge their "attitude" or emotional state. McNamara and Moreton (1995) contend that emotional and behavioural difficulties show up with children who are hurting, but don't know what to do with the pain. The Haukina Mai approach encourages teachers to learn the skills of connecting to the students' feelings, and dealing with them in a constructive manner.

Take this scenario: Quinton, aged 14, has a reputation as a tough student. He is often involved in fights with other students, and has been known to abuse teachers verbally. He is good at sport, particularly rugby league. He arrives at school on Monday morning eating a pie. He blatantly throws the paper bag on the ground. Here are three responses:

Response one: Pick up the paper please, Quinton.

Response two: Look here young man, you know we have a rule in this school about litter. Pick up that paper bag now, or else! Do you hear me?

Response three: Quinton, taihoa (wait a moment). The paper bag to the bin (pointing), thanks. Great league result for the Warriors on Saturday. How was your own form against Saint Paul's College?

The first response lacks assertiveness. Saying "please" at the end of the sentence appears to be a plea on the teacher's part, and the balance of power may sway in favour of the student. There is perhaps a 50/50 chance that Quinton will comply. The second response is not assertive, it is aggressive. It is also threatening. It is not hard to imagine the tone with which the "command" was uttered. Or else what? Detention? Principal's office? On report? It ends with a silly question which would allow Quinton a right of reply. The taste and the tenor of Quinton's reply might well take an already tentative situation to a level of intensity that both student and teacher may later regret. This may close the door on this student-teacher relationship, and therefore is contrary to the Huakina Mai approach. The odds that Quinton will comply in this instance are probably 10/90. The third response is both assertive and warm. Quinton's name is used up front, denoting a no-nonsense expression by the teacher. This teacher uses the pause and the gesture. It is highly likely that Quinton will comply, regardless of the conversation around sport. However, the third response demonstrates that the teacher knows the students and their interests. This teacher uses moderate language wisely. The third response is in line with the Huakina Mai strategy.

Take this scenario: Whaea Makere is a teacher of a Year 7 class in a decile two school with a large Māori population. She opens doorways in a similar way to a successful teacher (of mainly African-American students) in a study by Grace Stanford (1997), and to Bev Anaru in the Ngāti-Whakaue Enrichment Class. These teachers are passionate and believe that they can make a difference. They set high but attainable standards. They are aware of their role of promoting students' academic success. They are able to strike a balance between challenging students to learn difficult material, and at the same time enhancing their chances of success. Whaea Makere would say things like "Haere whakamua tonu (keep moving forward). I want you to have a go. Don't be afraid if you miss the point the first time. We fall down, we get up. Eventually we will get it right, we will get there and that is what matters. Haere whakamua . . ." Messages such as this, as well as Makere's attitude, encourage academic and social engagement in such a way that the self-esteem of the students in her class is enhanced. Whaea Makere's approach promotes the Huakina Mai principles.

The second step of the Hikairo approach is called "ihi", meaning assertiveness. Assertive communication, properly employed, is another effective strategy for responding to a student's unacceptable behaviour. Assertiveness refers to behaviour that enables people to act in their own best interests, to stand up for themselves without undue anxiety, to express honest feelings comfortably, or to exercise personal rights without denying the rights of others (Alberti and Emmons, 1986). For many years, Lee and Marlene Canter have been refining their Assertive Discipline system. Charles (1999) contends that they popularised the concepts of the rights that teachers and students have to a calm and safe environment. Earlier, they focused on teachers being strong leaders in the classroom. Their more recent emphasis is on the building of trusting and helpful relationships between teachers and students.

In the Māori world, kaumātua and kaikorero (orators) provide powerful models of assertiveness. On the marae, these orators excel in terms of self-expression, directness, and openness. They also excel in delivering messages rendered in the correct style for effective communication with people in a range of contexts. Assertive communication is an essential part of Māori protocol. According to Marsden (1975), ihi is a personal quality present in all human beings, but more developed in some than in others. The assertive quality of ihi can be a manifestation of a person's mana, so that mana is not simply a charisma, but also a force that can move people. Teachers whose behaviour reflects the quality of ihi, as well as those of aroha and manaaki, are more likely to succeed in establishing effective relationships with students and in managing behaviour in the classroom.

Acceptable behaviour must be taught and modelled. Lee and Marlene Canter (1992) say that students can't be expected to know automatically how to follow the direction of the many classroom activities. The best time for teaching directions is immediately prior to the first (or next) time the activity is to take place.

A small study involving 40 Māori students who gained high scores in School Certificate mathematics and science showed that teacher (and student) assertiveness was seen as a critical factor (Mitchell and Mitchell, 1988). While these students received a lot of encouragement from their parents, and had innate ability, they also worked hard and were competitive, and attempted to complete tasks and to make the completed task the best that it could be. These students had learned to be assertive about their approach to their education. Moreover, they recalled teachers who had high expectations of them, and who "pushed them". Further, this study referred to some Māori students who had not gone on to tertiary education. These students reported on negative experiences with teachers at school. It is obvious that some teachers have qualities of rangatiratanga and mana, and their approaches and strategies impact positively on Māori students in the classroom. Students talk about their teachers, sometimes glowingly, sometimes exasperatedly. To illustrate this, here is a simulated conversation between Marama and Janine in a secondary school playground about two teachers:

> Janine I hate going to Mr Macfarlane's classes. I can never understand the work he gives us. We are given worksheet after worksheet. I don't know why we do the mahi anyway, because he hardly ever marks it. It's boring there and koretake. He just lets us do what we like – man, he's a pushover.

> Marama Not like Whaea Makere, she's onto it. I got an A minus for my last assignment on "The history of Tarawera". Now I know heaps about the eruption in 1886, and about the destruction of the Pink and White Terraces. She said that next term we're going to do a study of Mokoia Island and a study of the life of Nelson Mandela. Whaea's pretty tough, works us hard eh. Her classes are tumeke.

Mr Macfarlane is koretake and lacking in rangatiratanga. Whaea Makere is like Bev Anaru, her rangatiratanga is beyond reproach. Whaea Makere's classroom management is a portrayal of quality pedagogy. Obviously, she is doing the things that Māori students (and all students) can understand, relate to, and learn from. Whaea Makere earns her rangatiratanga because she uses the following strategies:

- She pushes the students and she insists on quality work and is firm on task completion (i.e., works us hard).
- She has a no-nonsense approach to discipline (i.e., pretty tough).
- She is well-planned and projects towards the future (i.e., the studies next term).
- She allows students to explore local knowledge and icons (i.e., Tarawera Mountain and Mokoia Island), as well as studies of other nationalities (Nelson Mandela).

- She marks their work and gives informed and frequent feedback.

Rangatiratanga in the teaching and learning process is crucial for teachers when they have to analyse a situation that they must face, and to which they must respond. If teachers do not learn or take advantage of the body of knowledge on culturally inclusive pedagogy, then they limit their choices and inhibit their effectiveness in diverse classrooms. This section on rangatiratanga as an enabling element is intended to assist teachers in making decisions to enhance motivation for themselves and the students in their classrooms.

Cultural concept three: manaakitanga

Williams (1971) gives the meaning of manaaki as showing respect or kindness. Williams also refers to manaaki in terms of "to entertain", as in to be hospitable and kind to guests, to care for them. This is endorsed by Barlow (1993), who explains that the purpose of manaakitanga is to remind the host people that they should be kind to visitors who come to the marae. Barlow goes on to say that "the most important attributes for the hosts are to provide an abundance of food, a place to rest, and to speak nicely to visitors so that peace prevails during the gathering" (p. 63). For Ritchie (1992), manaakitanga is reciprocal, unqualified caring. In the reciprocal sense, Ritchie adds that "there is simply faith that one day that which one has contributed will be returned" (p. 75) and that "you are obliged to support, to care for, be concerned about, to feed, shelter and nurture your kin, and especially when they are in need . . . This is obligatory" (p. 78).

In attempting to advance these meanings into the domain of teaching and learning, manaakitanga can be taken to have several interpretations. The first is that teachers need to possess a range of strategies that will promote the caring process in the classroom (the metaphor of providing an abundance of food). Secondly, classrooms need to be culturally safe environments (the metaphor of providing a peaceful place). Thirdly, sound intercultural communication must prevail in the classroom (the metaphor of speaking nicely). Fourthly, manaakitanga is not optional, it is obligatory, and it has reciprocal ramifications, suggesting that teachers who value others will be valued in return (the metaphor of that which one has contributed being returned). There appear to be warnings here for teachers who disregard this notion of manaakitanga. These teachers' intolerances will inhibit their communicating interculturally, and reduce their effectiveness in the classroom.

In addition, manaakitanga is concerned with the head, as well as the heart. In terms of the heart, caring for students and colleagues is about compassion. In terms of the head, it is important for teachers to take stock of themselves in their personal and professional roles. I see this as teachers attempting to carry out their job with skill and grace, and in breathing life into their classrooms. This is about passion. To illustrate this, I will share two case studies of teachers whose cultures differed from that of most of their students, yet whose work among them was exemplary. Using their hearts and heads, they exuded compassion and passion.

Consider this: Turning teaching into "the life of Riley"

According to Rutter, Maugham, Mortimer, and Ouston (1979), a range of specific skills is demonstrated by effective teachers. They report on teachers who work at perfecting their craft. Smith and Laslett (1993) have also written about management rather than control of a classroom. They refer to management as skilled organisation and lesson presentation that actively engages the students in the learning. Actively engaged learning is a fundamental element of good teaching and learning identified by Māori students in the Te Kotahitanga Project (Bishop, Berryman, Richardson, and Tiakiwai, 2002). In other words, these teachers have to be fine technicians.

Exceptional teachers, however, have to be excellent communicators as well as fine technicians. To do this, the instruction has to be predicated on culturally responsive pedagogy. This has been described earlier as a style of teaching that takes into account students' cultural background, with respect to how they learn. This is not to be confused with deriving content from culture. Teaching African-American students about Martin Luther King Junior or teaching Māori students about the great Te Kooti is not necessarily culturally responsive, useful and worthwhile as these topics most surely are. Culturally responsive teaching is more about using the students' cultural experiences as a foundation upon which to develop knowledge and skills.

In previous chapters, we saw how Bev Anaru drew on the culture of her students to enhance their engagement. However, Bev was responsive to culture while maintaining the typical elements of more traditional successful classrooms. These typical elements include: having a structured curriculum; sustaining a challenging academic focus; having reasonable expectations of students' performance; insisting on quality in terms of producing the best that they can do; and emphasising crisp transitions from one activity to the next.

While Bev Anaru created an environment that encouraged and embraced culture at a primary school, I was privileged to observe a secondary school teacher who, like her, also developed a learning environment that was relevant to and respectful of the students' social and cultural experiences. This teacher was David Riley, non-Māori, aged 35, and in his fifth year of teaching at the time of my observations. The school he taught at was Tangaroa College. This college is a multicultural, coeducational state school of some 900 students, with a large Pasifika and Māori student representation.

For one day a week over a school term in 2001, I visited David's classroom. I was impressed with the structures in place and the general classroom orchestration. His meticulous planning and lesson momentum were underscored by manaakitanga. The students knew that they were valued, and because Māori and Pasifika students are keen to reciprocate their feelings, they valued David in return. Manaakitanga is manifested by creating an ethic of care in the classroom. David's class had posters on the walls that reflected the students' Polynesian community, their sporting icons, and the heroes and heroines that were known to them. David was also visible in the community, taking an active role in the homework centre at the Tupu Dawson Road Youth Library, attending sporting fixtures, shopping at the local supermarket, and attending the local church. He showed the students he cared by good teaching and a positive attitude.

As I observed David Riley at work in his classroom, I was struck by how his style bore a rather uncanny resemblance to the "four rules of classroom management" proposed by Smith and Laslett (1993). I list them here in a very abbreviated format, and with a slight modification to the original order:

• Get them in: greeting, seating, starting.
• Get on with it: content, manner.
• Get on with them: who's who, what's going on – knowing each child as an individual and reading the mood of the class as a whole.
• Move them on: closing and dismissing.

As each form class arrived, David usually waited near the doorway to greet them and direct them, if necessary, to a seating location. He advance organised and started promptly. Always well-planned, he knew his content well; his communication skills sent out messages that he was alert, and this kept the students attentive. David also maintained sound procedures for closing and dismissing. The way these four rules were played out was not identically applied to each of the classes he taught. The level of the class, and also the class personnel, were influential factors.

What else did David Riley do to show that he was genuine about sustaining manaakitanga with his secondary school classes? In what ways were messages of care extended to his students?

- He set goals that were realistic, and explained the rationale for the kaupapa.
- He set goals that could be accomplished, often within a reasonable time period. For some classes, a unit of study lasting six weeks was too long and drawn out. This presented the risk of the study losing its impetus, the students losing interest, and the teacher losing credibility.
- He reinforced little and often.
- He worked at the student's level, for example kneeling at the table and working with an individual student or a small group, while simultaneously scanning the room from time to time.
- He directed attention equitably. He avoided becoming too involved with one student for too long.
- He planned meticulously. This helped create a no-nonsense, task oriented ethos.
- He worked from a range of vantage points in the room, avoiding standing too often at the front or sitting behind his desk.
- He marked the students' work. Teachers who don't attend to this are sending out messages that they don't care! Where is the manaakitanga in that? What will that do to and for the teaching and learning dynamics?
- He used a vernacular that suited the context. From my experience, Māori students thrive on moderate language, balanced emotions, and clear explanations. Going berserk is out of kilter with the concept of manaakitanga. If that is the case, what is the point in raving on? Try . . . "I am disappointed with your behaviour, Maru. I like you, Maru, but I don't like your behaviour. Kia mau."
- He had a principal, Mike Leach, who took an active role in encouraging David, and the rest of his staff, to develop their careers as educators of a diverse cohort of students. To this end, regular whole-staff professional development courses were provided. Like Terry Morrison of Ngongotahā School, Mike Leach maintained a high degree of visibility around the school. During my time at Tangaroa College, Mike was seen to be visiting classrooms

frequently. When he visited David's classes, I noticed the appreciation (or respect, or both), that the students had for a principal who cared. This principal knew what manaakitanga meant, so he affected it.

I will now turn to the study of a teacher in North America. While geographically and contextually different from David Riley's situation at Tangaroa College, the similarities in terms of bringing about the presence of manaakitanga are pronounced.

Consider this: It is not so much cultural compatibility that is required in diverse classrooms – it is cultural connectedness that counts

Cecelia Pierce (1996) reports a case study showing how one effective teacher, teaching primarily at-risk learners, created a classroom climate that enhanced learner outcomes. Pierce, of the University of Alabama, centred her study on Mary Morgan (not her real name), a white middle-school teacher with 24 years of teaching experience. Her effectiveness in teaching at-risk students was determined by the recommendations of teachers, administrators, parents, and former students. Pierce observed Mary Morgan daily for 12 weeks in her classroom, and recorded audiotapes and field notes. The researcher especially cited verbal and non-verbal teaching behaviours and patterns, teacher personality characteristics, and the way in which these factors facilitated student learning.

The inner-city school in this study was located in the southeastern United States, where the student population was predominantly black. The class included 21 students; 29 percent were white, and 71 percent were black. Seventeen of the students had been identified as at-risk by the guidance counsellors and the teacher, based on their low income family network and previous school performance. Pierce (1996) presumed that the majority of these students did not see the benefit of education reflected in their parents. Consequently, they exhibited qualities of hesitancy, fear, and insecurity when confronted with the demands of school, an observation shared by researchers in other settings (Ashman and Elkins, 1998; Clark et al., 1996; Kauffman, 1997; McInerney and McInerney, 1998). These attributes, Morgan maintained, needed to be countered and minimised by developing a classroom ambience which diminished the threat of failure, allowed opportunity for student participation in the learning process, and provided a safe haven for students. Pierce (1996) identified three key components in Mary Morgan's classroom which gave it "safe haven" status:

- a classroom organisation based upon correct standards of behaviour and a sensitivity toward others;
- a variety of roles assumed by the teacher to give support to the students; and
- the teacher's enthusiasm for the students.

The chief beliefs and practices which underpinned these components are outlined in Table 8.1 below.

Table 8.1

Key components of the "safe haven" status of Mary Morgan's classroom

Pierce (1996) concludes that Mary Morgan's classroom climate was created primarily through specific behaviours, which nurtured the emotional needs of her students. Her planned intention to set the scene at the beginning of the year proved to be both proactive and preventative.

Mary Morgan, not unlike David Riley and Bev Anaru, allowed students to thrive because the environments were safe, predictable, and non-hostile.

Roles Assumed by the Teacher	Classroom Organisation	Teacher's Enthusiasm for Students
• Teacher modelled the desired behaviour. • Teacher as person, encourager, counsellor, and safety net. • Teacher might share, discerningly, his or her own experiences. • Teacher was never threatening. • Teacher skilled both in academic and non-academic dialogue.	• Instilled in students a belief in their abilities to learn and a desire to achieve. • Each child knew they were valued. • Planned to bond into a co-operative unit at beginning of year. • Ensured students understood and internalised the rules. • Explained consequences of improper behaviour.	• Enthusiasm was developed from life experiences. • Enthusiasm was developed from formal education experiences. • Relaxed classroom atmosphere added to enthusiastic climate. • Freedom of (but controlled) movement within the classroom. • Teacher's attention to students. • Teacher's warm smile.

(Pierce, 1996)

Where possible, learning was linked to the real world and to the culture of the students. These teachers challenged students in terms of articulating achievement, responsibility, and persistence. That appeared to be their way of making educational meaning of the concept of manaakitanga.

Cultural concept four: kotahitanga

Essentially, kotahitanga embellishes the notions of unity and bonding, practices that were fundamental to tipuna. Traditionally, Māori lived in close knit communities and worked together and planted food together. Everybody contributed to the well-being of the tribe. "One of the reasons for unity was to give everyone an equal share of the resources so that no one suffered unduly . . . The concept of unity pervaded every aspect of tribal functions and activities" (Barlow, 1993, p. 57). Ritchie (1992) has similar perceptions, chiefly that kotahitanga is the process of becoming one out of many. It is the process of recognising everyone's mana, and of bringing a sense of unity to a specific context (for example, whānau, parish, school, classroom). The process of reaching consensus is not simple, and it can be of considerable duration. Hapū from within my own iwi, and the iwi itself, have records of many arguments and tensions. The Te Arawa canoe's voyage records disagreements between two of its foremost leaders. In this historical situation, as with many situations in contemporary Māori society, a balance was worked through so that opposites were overcome by unity.

Kotahitanga, in educational terms, means taking an inclusive approach to classroom management and discipline, so that the bonding process brings everyone to understand each other in the day-to-day classroom activities on the one hand, and in dealing with disciplinary concerns on the other. Let us now consider several suggestions for attempting to make kotahitanga work in each of these areas – classroom strategies, and positive discipline. Note the use of the word "attempting". One must maintain a level of discretion, because despite planning to teach good work habits and social behaviours, students may not buy into this. Cummings (2000) reminds educators that in this highly technological world, teachers have strong competition for student attention and habits. Behaviours modelled on television, in movies, and at sporting venues have desensitised students to violence and antisocial behaviours. How can teachers compete with the media, the movies, and the visibility of the gangs? This competition certainly makes a teacher's job more demanding – but teachers can still make a difference!

Consider this: Give whole-class rewards

Sonja Bateman (Ngai Tahu) is the District Māori Advisor for Group Special Education Waikato. She offers the following explanation and example, which illustrate both collective responsibility and individual mana in the one scenario.

It is well known that operating a whole-class reward system helps create a cohesion (kotahitanga) and overall team spirit within the class, if implemented with integrity. It can be used to acknowledge a predetermined range of desirable behaviours that are being displayed en masse, or class-wide. Such a system can be tailored in order to achieve ongoing and/or specified longer term goals. Every member of the class has the opportunity to contribute to the team success, to share in the rewards, and to thus feel a valued part of the team. A whole-class reward system also promotes behaviours such as "awhi" (helping) and "tautoko" (support), as it relies primarily on positive peer pressure. If used properly and contingently, this system is also able to be used to raise the mana (status) of less popular students: the teacher needs to "read" the timing opportunities that arise intermittently, and pounce on these moments.

Here is an example from actual classroom experience. A class "mushroom" was drawn up on the whiteboard: the goal was for the whole class to earn a specified number of spots on the mushroom for a range of desirable behaviours (e.g., being ready for work, speaking politely, helping each other, tidying up. . . .). On achieving the target, the class would be able to participate in some pre-determined and agreed rewards (e.g., baking, playing a game, watching a video, painting the windows, going for a swim, etc.).

One particular boy in a class I once taught, Liam, was not very popular, probably on account of his tendency to unknowingly offer untimely and inappropriate comments from time to time (as part of his attempts to socialise), which would ultimately invite rejection from his peers. Their response would then cause Liam to withdraw socially until he had summoned up enough courage to try again. Consequently, making friends was not an easy thing for him to do: he did not interact very well with other students, which meant that sharing and bonding with his peers were quite alien concepts to him. Interestingly, Liam was fully aware of his lack of friends, and was saddened and confused by the situation. It obviously appeared to him that no matter how hard he tried to connect with his peers the worse things became for him. I had noticed that his attempts to reach out to his peers were decreasing in number, and the social withdrawal was increasing, giving very real cause for concern. Fortunately Liam liked to please me, his teacher, as most kids do, and would often come and talk to me.

Considering the concerns I had regarding Liam's status as a class member, I made the decision to "manipulate" the whole-class reward system a little, in order to raise Liam's mana. The class needed 25 spots on the mushroom, and had achieved 24. I intentionally dragged out the attainment of the prized final spot. The class as a whole were really keen to get there and were trying particularly hard to nab that last spot on the mushroom. I took Liam aside and asked him, quite unobtrusively, to do a particular task . . . "Liam, it would be great if you could tidy up the art supplies at the back of the room, thanks". He was more than happy to do so. When he had finished doing this I publicly announced "Hey, thanks Liam, you have done something for the whole class. You showed us the importance of keeping our room tidy. Well done. For that I am going to put the last spot on the mushroom." That scenario was a win-win situation for all, but significantly more so for Liam, as it meant he received a great deal of praise and positive feedback from his peers. It also strengthened my relationship with Liam. Sure I was being mischievous, but that was part of the strategy . . .

Consider this: Do a class study on the Treaty of Waitangi

Hardman, Drew, and Egan (1999) contend that at school, young people's thoughts and feelings about diverse cultures are at least partially shaped by what they learn in the classroom. Incomplete information, stereotypical presentations about different cultures, or lack of full participation of minority groups in the classroom detract from gaining an understanding or appreciation about cultures that characterise New Zealand. Neglectful or careless treatment of this important topic has the potential to perpetuate eurocentric notions. A more complete education, according to Hardman et al. (1999), must include recognition of the role of the cultures, and in particular, as far as this country is concerned, the role of the two Treaty partners. If the Treaty of Waitangi were acknowledged in the true spirit of its intentions—an agreement of two peoples to bond as one nation—intercultural communication in this country would be immensely more wholesome than it is. While I vehemently believe that every teacher must have a sound knowledge and understanding of the Treaty, exposing students to New Zealand's founding document would also have benefits in terms of improving intercultural communication. In a school at which she was teaching, Sonja Bateman wanted to establish kotahitanga in her Year 7 class very early in term one (remember that Mary Morgan bonded early with her class as well). The following account explains how Sonja carried out a unit of study with her class.

Having a "class treaty" is an excellent way of creating kotahitanga and group accountability within a classroom. Waitangi Day falls within the first fortnight or so of the school year, and the unit of study that is delivered on that kaupapa provides teachers with a timely opportunity for experiencing what a treaty actually means, why it is valued, and what is involved in putting together a treaty. In my classroom I would draw out the positives of having a treaty, and together we would discuss these ideas. Further, I would put forward the idea of having a class treaty. I would ask the students to think about what details we might need to consider. With careful prompting (persuasive guidance?) they would mention such things as rights and responsibilities, honesty, care, consideration, respect, and so forth. We would brainstorm these ideas on the whiteboard, and we would group the words under the two key themes, namely rights and responsibilities. These themes can be paralleled in many ways to the Treaty of Waitangi articles of partnership, protection and participation. I would ask questions when it came to the point of shaping these themes into the final treaty format – for example: "When we come to school each day and into this classroom, what rights do we have?" And, "So, to help make these rights real, what do we need to do? What responsibilities do we have?"

Treaty of Room 17:

In Room 17 . . .

1. We have rights: these include the right to be taught, the right to learn, the right to be respected, the right to be included, the right to feel safe.

2. We have responsibilities: these include the need to be respectful of others (their feelings, their learning time, and their possessions), to be honest, to help care for each other, to look after our environment, to use polite language, to work hard, and to "have a go".

I would then put together a draft treaty document (with the word DRAFT written at the top), which was passed around everyone in the classroom, so that they could check that what I had recorded was a true and fair account of what had previously been discussed. This approach had the potential to be a powerful stage in the process, as it showed the students that I wanted everyone to understand what they were agreeing to, and it also indicated that some genuine power-sharing was occurring. I would talk to the students about the importance of knowing what they were going to sign. This would lead on to a discussion that perhaps this was one reason why the Treaty of Waitangi has had such a turbulent history . . . both sides could not agree on the intent of the document that they had signed independently. More talk would be generated on how this lack of understanding might inhibit intercultural communication now, as it did in 1840. Did Room 17 want to get it right? Yes.

When the final wording for the treaty was agreed upon, it would be written up on an A2 sheet and passed around for everyone to sign, myself included. I would mention to the class that teachers also learn from students, daily, as a consequence of classroom interactions (the concept of ako was imparted at this point). The idea of actually signing something was significant. The fact that their signatures were valued had somewhat of a wry appeal to the students. Many of them spent time practising their signatures over and over before signing the final treaty version!

The treaty would then be laminated and displayed on the wall. This was a useful document in terms of keeping students on track with their learning and behaviour. Sometimes, when tension threatened, a subtle reference to our agreement was often the mechanism to return calm to the environment. I would also mention the treaty in other contexts – praise them when they were working well, by pointing to the treaty and saying "It's great to see how we are all keeping to our word – excellent work people". The fact that they had "promised" certain things, by the very act of signing their name, was an extremely powerful tool, and it reminded the students about trust, honesty, and accountability. Not unlike other classroom management strategies, I had to avoid satiation. Too much of the same will lead to loss of meaningfulness. Sometimes allowing a strategy a state of lag is a clever ploy, as this prevents staleness or ineffectiveness setting in. Macfarlane (2003) insists that proportionality is vital in classroom management. That was the case here as we sought kotahitanga for Room 17.

Consider this: Person-to-person bonding

Taking time to bond with students, to win them over, is the first step in classroom management. Diero (cited in Cummings, 2000) studied how teachers form healthy connections with junior high school students, and identified these strategies:
- creating one-to-one time with students;
- using appropriate self-disclosure;
- networking with family and friends;
- building a sense of community in the classroom; and
- using rituals and traditions.

Examples of these strategies have appeared elsewhere in this chapter. For instance, I referred to the fact that many teachers have students study whakapapa at the beginning of the year. Bear in mind that the first thing to know about the students is their names. Pronunciation of Māori names must be correct, even if the teacher has to work hard at getting it right. To call a girl Rangi-Maree rather than Rangimarie is unacceptable, as is Roi-marty for Roimata. Rangimarie means peace or tranquillity, Roimata means tears. These two names, like all names, whether Māori or non-Māori, have a history and meaning to them that may go back generations. Displaying the names of each student with photos can be a good prompt for teachers to learn who's who early on in the year.

Appropriate self-disclosure is another helpful expression of teacher-student bonding, as it is an act of the teacher sharing feelings and experiences within a climate of trust. This has to be carried out with care. Naturally, there are some experiences and feelings one would never disclose. Kenny Rogers, the country and western balladeer, has the right advice with these lyrics: "You gotta know when to hold, and know when to fold."

Many teachers I know use a number of interesting rituals and traditions. Here are two of these:

Mihi in the morning ritual

Insist on a brief mihi (kia ora, morena, ata marie, good morning) during pastoral time before period one. This is good from the point of view of practising aroha (common courtesy). It is also good in terms of allowing the teacher to observe the ahua (attitude) of the student. Many students arrive at school deprived of sleep, hungry, unwashed, angry, and so forth. If these symptoms and conditions go unnoticed, problems could escalate as the day progresses. The ritual of the mihi would prompt the teacher to get in early to address the situation. Most teachers would prefer to buy a pie for the student to suppress the hunger, or have a korero (in moderate language) . . . "Matiu, I have a couple of minutes now. It looks like you have something on your mind. Let's share it, just you and me. Kei te pai." Good teachers manage these situations with little ado, and with little expense in terms of money or time. Spending two dollars for a pie or five minutes for a korero would be a good investment.

Homework in the afternoon ritual

The second ritual to consider is that of homework. Many primary school classrooms have a homework tradition that encourages younger children to read every night.

Homework does not have to be a solitary activity. My mokopuna, who recently had his sixth birthday, regularly chooses to read to one or both of his parents, and the parents reciprocate by reading to him. Many middle schools and secondary schools are also finding value in establishing homework centres for after school. Teachers often report on how Māori students appreciate the camaraderie, the kai that is often provided, and the help they receive from teachers who sincerely have their interests at heart. The "Goodman-Fielder Composite School of the Year 2002", Clover Park Middle School in Otara, has found that providing students with the opportunity to remain after school, where they work and socialise together, an effective kotahitanga strategy. Principal Ann Milne is adamant that students should express their Māoriness at school, knowing full well that these students bring their Māoriness with them, into the school. She believes in "pushing the students, academically, socially, and culturally", and she is fully supportive of maximising the availability of school resources in order to enhance this development. Many students opt to stay at school and "get their homework done", and there are a number of reasons for this. At school, a range of resources is available to them – for instance, computers with free link to the internet, appropriate literature, the required stationery, and teachers right there if required. This practice is seen as a natural extension of the genuine cultural ecology that permeates their environment. In the school's small senior class, these practices have supported the students in their endeavours to pass their respective levels of the National Certificate of Educational Achievement (NCEA) qualification. So, for these Clover Park students, this aspect of kotahitanga supports their school learning, their knowledge of themselves, and their sense of place, as Māori, within the broader context of their lives.

Consider this: Set up "te wiki o te reo Māori" as a whole school approach

Māori language week in this country has often borne the brunt of massive criticism, primarily for the tokenistic reputation that it has acquired. Rightly or wrongly, it has been part of mainstream educational practice in this country for many years. In the late 1980s, I facilitated a Māori language "fortnight" programme at an intermediate school. Because the composite classes covered only two years, and the intercommunication system throughout the school was of a sound technical quality, it was possible to do the learning and teaching of te reo me ona tikanga (Māori language and customs) with the entire school population, together. This involved the principal and school managers, the classroom teachers, and the 400 students. I planned the activities for the students and the instructions for teachers, so that everyone was an active participant. Each day between 1.05 and 1.45, the intercommunication system would burst into life in every classroom of the school. It went something like this:

1.05 – 1.10   Tauparapara: Brief introduction by facilitator
Mihi: Brief whaikōrero by one of the staff.

1.10 – 1.20   Te reo Māori: Oral language practice. Teachers would have many of the sentences written up on the board so that students could follow the words.

1.20	Tuhituhi Māori: Writing Māori words and prose about Māori tikanga, using prepared worksheets.
1.30	Local Māori sportsperson or leader addresses the school.
1.35 – 1.45	Waiata – song, whole school singing together but from their respective classrooms.
	Billy T. joke – the students loved the humour.
	Whakakapi – bringing the session to closure.

One runs the risk of being criticised for perpetuating a "tokenism" slant, perhaps, for this type of approach, but at that time it was a whole school approach that worked. The teachers applied themselves rigorously to the planning, preparation, teaching, and evaluation. In reviewing the study, staff reported on the success as well as the concerns they had identified. They posed questions such as: What did we learn from this experience? What might we change if we were to do it again? How did the experience affect the students' and staff's understandings and interests? In addition students were enthused. Learning some reo and tikanga occurred, where under regular circumstances it may not have done so. Intercultural communication broke out too. This is not an approach that all schools would be able to or willing to implement, for wide-ranging reasons. It is merely another suggestion to put on the table.

Consider this: Take a traditional Māori discipline approach to conferencing – te hui whakatika

Culture plays an extremely important part in student conferencing. People from one ethnic background are likely to go into a conferencing situation with very different views and expectations from people who come from another ethnic background. Conferencing is not new to Māori people. Traditional Māori societies had this down to a fine art, and many examples are manifested magnificently in mythology, legends, and history. Contemporary Māori society has retained an abundance of what tipuna (ancestors) had to offer, despite the infiltration of western processes on conferencing techniques. For Māori, oneness of tinana, hinengaro and wairua is often perceived as a distinction from the rationality and logic that influence conferencing from a western perspective. Māori rationale and logic need to be embraced if the conferencing process is going to be of value to troubled Māori rangatahi.

Four quintessential features illustrating traditional Māori discipline were identified by Olsen, Maxwell, and Morris (cited in McElrea, 1994). They were:

- an emphasis upon reaching consensus and involving the whole community;
- a desired outcome of reconciliation, and a settlement acceptable to all parties, rather than the isolation and punishment of the offender;
- not to apportion blame, but to examine the wider reason for the wrong, with an implicit assumption that there was often wrong on both sides; and
- less concern with whether or not there had been a breach of law, and more concern with the restoration of harmony.

These traditional Māori discipline procedures underpin a "model of healing" adopted by Professor Michael Brown when he was Chief Judge of the Children's and Young Persons' Court. In 1998 I modified the model (see Figure 8.1), with Professor Brown's permission, so it could be used as a hui whakatika (collaborative restoration of mana) in disciplinary procedures in middle schools and secondary schools.

The hui, while bearing some resemblance to a Family Group Conference (FGC), is also distinct, because aspects of Māoritanga are given authentic appreciation. No long-term suspension or expulsion would be possible without first holding such a hui. The hui would involve the student and the significant people in his or her educational and community life. It should include any person who had been a particular victim of the misconduct (Macfarlane, cited in Fraser, Moltzen, and Ryba, 2000). Furthermore, there must be clear processes for the participation of whānau in the provision of educational services. Thought needs to be given to linking with Māori institutions, and the extent of the role of these associations. The New Zealand Māori Wardens Association, Mātua Whāngai, and the Mokoia Wānanga are admirable institutions whose services to education are of the highest order. There are numerous others.

Figure 8.1

A Model of Healing by Judge Michael Brown (1998)

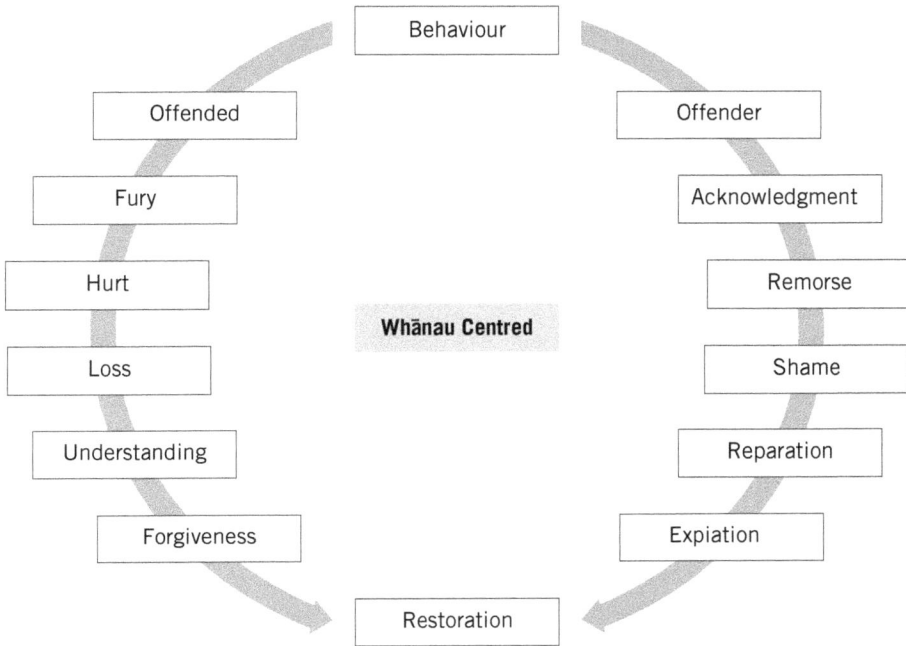

Behaviour

Offended

Offender

Fury

Acknowledgment

Hurt

Remorse

Whānau Centred

Loss

Shame

Understanding

Reparation

Forgiveness

Expiation

Restoration

Adapted by Macfarlane (cited in Fraser, Moltzen, and Ryba, 2000, p. 90)

While I cannot go into a full and thorough description of the hui whakatika in this chapter, an actual case study I facilitated using this model appears in Chapter 4 of Learners with Special Needs in Aotearoa New Zealand (Fraser, Moltzen, and Ryba, 2000). This case study describes the importance of pre-hui meetings, the rituals applicable to the hui itself, and how a plan can be developed and a re-storying process can be achieved by way of kotahitanga.

Because this is an ecological approach to discipline, the group at the hui would consider all the relevant matters and then draw up a plan to address these concerns. McElrea (1996) contends that a good plan would involve some items for the school's benefit (e.g., non-violence pacts, attendance undertakings), some items for the students' benefit (e.g., joining a sports club, counselling), some items for the benefit of the community (e.g., removal of graffiti) and some items for the benefit of the whānau (e.g., father to take active interest in school community).

The hui is an art, in that while it subscribes to prescriptions and routines, it is also influenced by qualities and contingencies that are unpredictable. All those present at the hui find themselves being drawn into this "whānau of interest" (Bishop and Glynn, 1999), and the ends that the meeting achieves are often created in the process. There is an analogy here to Eisner's (1994) "four senses of the art of teaching", where he proposes that teaching can be an aesthetic experience, heuristic, adventitious, and emergent. Hui—genuine hui—take on all of those qualities. Educators need to address these issues in a culturally inclusive way and, if the time and context determines, move away from the sometimes mechanical Individual Education Plan (IEP) and FGC. The Hui Whakatika, with its emphasis on kotahitanga and the other core cultural concepts, is more fair and equitable for Māori students and whānau than the conventional disciplinary meetings.

Cultural concept five: Pumanawatanga

Often, when speakers refer to the tribe to which I belong, they say, "Ko Te Arawa e waru pumanawa", meaning that they acknowledge the eight beating hearts of the hapū of the Te Arawa iwi. I have chosen this as the final and central cultural concept, so as to draw the analogy of the classroom and school as being dynamic and alive. The concept of pumanawatanga extends outwards to breathe life into whanaungatanga, rangatiratanga, manaakitanga, and kotahitanga, which are themselves interconnected. Pumanawatanga is a reference to school tone, classroom morale, and teacher attitude. The cultural concepts referred to in this chapter are the seeds from which classroom management strategies grow and culturally relevant pedagogy is realised. The educultural wheel (see Figure 8.2) situates pumawatanga at the hub; it then ripples out to all of its surrounds.

Figure 8.2

The Educultural Wheel

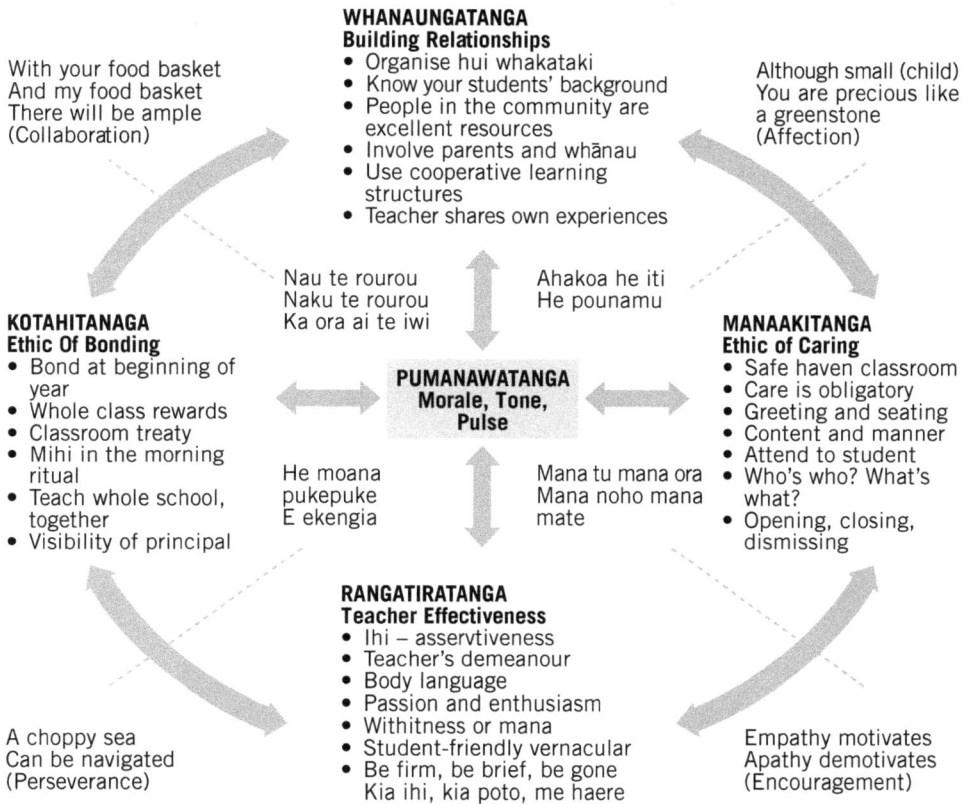

With your food basket
And my food basket
There will be ample
(Collaboration)

WHANAUNGATANGA
Building Relationships
- Organise hui whakataki
- Know your students' background
- People in the community are excellent resources
- Involve parents and whānau
- Use cooperative learning structures
- Teacher shares own experiences

Although small (child)
You are precious like
a greenstone
(Affection)

Nau te rourou
Naku te rourou
Ka ora ai te iwi

Ahakoa he iti
He pounamu

KOTAHITANAGA
Ethic Of Bonding
- Bond at beginning of year
- Whole class rewards
- Classroom treaty
- Mihi in the morning ritual
- Teach whole school, together
- Visibility of principal

PUMANAWATANGA
Morale, Tone, Pulse

MANAAKITANGA
Ethic of Caring
- Safe haven classroom
- Care is obligatory
- Greeting and seating
- Content and manner
- Attend to student
- Who's who? What's what?
- Opening, closing, dismissing

He moana
pukepuke
E ekengia

Mana tu mana ora
Mana noho mana
mate

RANGATIRATANGA
Teacher Effectiveness
- Ihi – asservtiveness
- Teacher's demeanour
- Body language
- Passion and enthusiasm
- Withitness or mana
- Student-friendly vernacular
- Be firm, be brief, be gone
  Kia ihi, kia poto, me haere

A choppy sea
Can be navigated
(Perseverance)

Empathy motivates
Apathy demotivates
(Encouragement)

© Macfarlane, (2003)

Infusing these five cultural concepts and strategies is likely to have a positive effect on students' learning and on teachers' teaching, because cultural referents are employed. Acknowledging these cultural referents and employing a culturally relevant pedagogy will signal to Māori students that their culture matters. Such an approach offers students a presence of what is familiar, in terms of their Māoritanga and Pākehātanga. If the learning and teaching connect with the cultures represented in the classroom, the students are more likely to "switch on". That is how critical the role of the teacher is.

Although the Ministry of Education is to be applauded for regularly raising the issue of recruiting more Māori teachers, I believe that the call needs to be broadened, so that more emphasis is placed on diverse pedagogies in both pre-service courses and in-service professional development provision. Too many teachers know too little about what a Māori worldview is. Too many teachers know too little about what culturally relevant pedagogy is. This does not make them ineffective teachers, because most of them are highly effective practitioners. The reality is that if they listened to culture, as Bev Anaru, Mary Morgan, and David Riley did, more and more teachers would be more culturally competent. The ideas in this book are not going to convert teachers into becoming ultra-successful in diverse settings, nor were they intended to do that. The intention was to share some educultural notions and concepts, along with some educultural stories.

CHAPTER NINE

Cultural centredness

On the basis of observations of the Ngāti-Whakaue Enrichment Class, along with those strategies that stem from the cultural concepts outlined in this chapter, it is argued here that a central characteristic of programmes that attend successfully to Māori students' achievement is cultural centredness. Significant aspects of that cultural-centredness have been outlined. It is argued that these aspects are fundamental to the process of "restorying" that is critical to the success of many Māori students (Macfarlane, 2002).

According to Bishop and Glynn (1999), power sharing is a necessary condition for relationship-based pedagogies. Interactions involve sequential revisiting of experiences and their cultural meanings, in ways that encourage teachers and students to become committed both to one another and to the learning process. This book has been a narrative of relationship-based pedagogies. The original story began by discovering the classroom dynamics of a humble setting within Ngongotahā School. The story was made possible by a school principal's vision, the mentoring of senior staff, an exceptional teacher, the whānau community of the Ngāti-Whakaue Enrichment Class, and an iwi entity which does not hold back on resources for promising initiatives.

Alive in every culture is a rich and vibrant tradition of storytelling. Shared within families and communities, stories often serve to anchor and enrich human pathways. For example, historians of the Te Arawa tribe tell of the time when Ngāti Ohomairangi (the parent tribe in the distant homeland of Hawaiki) decided that the time had arrived to migrate to new homes and islands that were less crowded. At that time, Ngatoroirangi was the high priest of the principal tribe, of which Ngāti Ohomairangi was a division. Houmaitawhiti was the paramount chief of Ngāti Ohomairangi, and the tribal priests were two brothers, Tia and Hei. When it came time for Ngāti Ohomairangi to move on, the canoe builders were assembled, the commander of the Te Arawa canoe being Tamatekapua. According to Stafford (1967) and Grace, (cited in Macfarlane, 2002), Tamatekapua was a chief who was endowed with great courage and prowess, one who possessed a gift for leadership which raised him to pre-eminence in the tribe. Tradition indicates that he was, at times, mischievous. Nonetheless, his boldness and strong personality won him the loyalty, affection, and admiration of his people. Tamatekapua is the ancestor of the Te Arawa tribe. His memory is preserved for all to see in the beautifully carved and ornamented meeting house of the same name at Ohinemutu, Rotorua (Grace, 1995). In hearing stories of this kind, young Māori learn that they, too, have a place in history and tradition, a place that provides security and continuity.

The unfolding of history is fraught with intrigue and wonder. Not all such stories settle peacefully in our ears, our hearts, and our minds. Nevertheless, whether we weep, or laugh, or become quietly meditative, these stories are part of our past and give us a sense of identity and continuity. Thus, according to Robinson and Ginter (1999), all such stories can serve as gifts for the present if we are open to these gifts.

Narrative pedagogies are a means of providing and creating power-sharing relationships in classrooms. Bishop and Glynn (1999) propose that the aim of narratives as pedagogy is to create, in the minds of those who are participants in the pedagogic process, "an image of relationships that are committed, connected and participatory . . . and where possible an holistic approach to curriculum is fundamental to the practices developed" (p. 176). Students who have had negative experiences are unlikely to revise their views of themselves and of their potential simply because they are not invited to do so by their teachers. If, however, their experiences of themselves, of others, and of the learning environment become positive, then it becomes possible for them to believe that it is reasonable to revise these views. Hence, sound pedagogy which is relationship-based is critical to the process of restorying. It is suggested that there are five key elements to culturally sound pedagogy:
- adopting a dual emphasis – social and academic;
- engaging students in studying local wisdom, reo and tikanga, as well as global knowledge;

- promoting an approach which is participatory and engaging;
- becoming involved holistically through style, spirit, and content; and
- drawing from theory, ancient or contemporary or both, to enrich practice.

Table 9.1 outlines four compelling facets which help explain how experiences at the Ngāti-Whakaue Enrichment Class at Ngongotahā School were key sources of knowledge that were transpositioned into sound pedagogical practices.

Table 9.1

Aspects of the programme at Ngongotahā School's Ngāti-Whakaue Enrichment Class

Compelling Sources	Transforming Knowledge into Practice
Skilled leadership	Has respect for Māori knowledge, language and customs Manifests qualities of tika, pono, aroha and ihi (Tate, 1990) Is consistent and credible Appeals to the best in each person
Home, school, and community links	Reach out to community Encourage community to reach in (McKinley, 2002) View the notion of whānau as paramount (Smith, 1992) Hold frequent "open days"
Roles assumed by teachers	Models the desired behaviour (Glynn, 1998) Shows skill in Māori communication, has cultural competence (Hohepa, 1999) Is an intercultural communicator Raises students' achievement academically, socially, culturally
Style adopted by teachers	Democratic and authoritative Participatory and engaging (Bishop and Glynn, 1999) Holistic and flexible (Pere, 1994) Assertive and warm (Macfarlane, 1997)

The Ngāti-Whakaue Enrichment Class was observed to be succeeding in providing a culturally responsive model of learning and teaching. As a model, it held a belief that the curriculum should affirm the validity and legitimacy of Māori knowledge and culture by acknowledging the importance of Māori metaphors, concepts, and principles. The effect of this was observed to be the type of restorying that is often so fundamental to students tasting success.

Overall, the educational experiences observed in the Ngāti-Whakaue Enrichment Class provide some responses to issues relating to Māori student and whānau perceptions of school. This site, like many other successful educational contexts in New Zealand and around the world, provides a platform for educators to begin to see how it is possible to "listen to culture". It is hoped that those involved in the professional practice of teaching will seek to refine their approaches by learning more about diverse groups through professional development, research dissemination, and fully inclusive practices (Cross, Bazron, Dennis, and Isaacs, 1989). This may require boldness and a strong will. But remember, the renowned ancestor Tamatekapua had strength of character, strength of personality, and a tendency to take risks . . . which won him the affection and admiration of his people.

GLOSSARY

ako	literally to learn, and to teach. The reciprocity of a person being both a learner and a teacher according to the teaching/learning context.
Aotearoa	New Zealand
aroha	love
awhi	help, support
ata marie	nice morning
e hika	affectionate salutation
hapū	clan, sub-tribe
hinengaro	mind
hōhā	frustration, form of mischievousness
hongi	the "pressing of noses" as a greeting, denotes well-being and acceptance
huakina	open
hui	literally a meeting, a gathering wherein certain rituals apply
hūmarietanga	genuineness, denoting strength through calmness
ihi	assertiveness, firmness
iwi	tribe

kai	food
kaiārahitanga	leadership
kaikōrero	people involved in discussions relating to a particular event
kanohi ki te kanohi	face-to-face interchanges
kapahaka	ritual dance
karakia	prayer
kaumātua	respected older person(s)
kaupapa Māori	Māori philosophy and principles
kaupapa	philosophy, theme, content
kawanatanga	administrative control
kī mai	tell me
kia hiwa ra	be alert
kia manawanui	be stout-hearted
kia mau	pay attention
kia ora	general greeting or acknowledgment
kia poto	be brief
Kingitanga	the protocols and beliefs of the King Movement
koha	traditional Māori gifting
kōhanga reo	language nest, preschool teaching through the medium of Māori
koretake	not good, unacceptable
koroua	respected older Māori male
kotahitanga	unity, togetherness, bonding
kuia	respected older Māori female
kura kaupapa Māori	primary school (Year 1–8) teaching through Māori-medium
kura	school
mahi	task, work

mana atua	the power of the gods
mana mātauranga	literally means, the power of education. In this context it is used to explain the notion of the reality of education (epistemology) within a Māori context.
mana tangata	the power of the individual
mana tīpuna	the power of ancestors
mana whenua	the power of the land
mana	prestige, divine right, influence, status, identity, power, authority
manaaki	to care for, show respect, hospitality
manaakitanga	the ethic of caring
Māori	indigenous people of New Zealand
Māoritanga	the way of life, the principles of living that encapsulates "being Māori"
marae	Māori community setting
mātauranga Māori	Māori knowledge
mātauranga	education, knowledge
matua	older male; respectful title for an older male
mau taiaha	traditional weaponry art
me haere	be gone
mokopuna	grandchildren, or children of that generation but not necessarily the children from a direct line, rather children who have some affiliation with the older person
mōrena	good morning
ngākautanga	coming from the heart
Pākehā	literally a non-Māori, European
Pākehātanga	Europeanness
poukai	Tainui Kingitanga ritual

pūmanawa	beating heart
pūmanawatanga	pulsation
pūrākau	story, legend
rangatahi	youth
rangimārie	peace, tranquility
raupatu	land confiscations
Ringatū	religious movement, the "up-raised hand"
roimata	tears
taihoa	wait a moment
tamariki	children
tangata whenua	people of the land, indigenous people
taonga	treasure
tauparapara	chant to start a speech
tautoko	commitment, to second, support
Te Aho Matua	ancient philosophies
Te Arawa	canoe and tribe in Bay of Plenty
Te Kōhanga Reo	see kōhanga reo
te reo	the language
te reo Māori	the Māori language
tika	justice
tika tēnā	that's right
tikanga Māori	aspects of Māori culture
tikanga	cultural pattern, custom, obligations, and conditions
tinana	body, physical domain
tino rangatiratanga	literally means chiefly control, metaphorically self-determination
tipuna	ancestor
tonu	keep going, continue

tuakana	older, senior
tuhituhi	write
Tū-mata-uenga	god of war
tumeke	choice, great
waiata	song, chant
wairua	spirit
wairuatanga	spirituality
waka	canoe
wānanga	traditional Māori learning centre
whaikōrero	oratory
whakakapi	wrap-up, as in proceedings; closing comments
whakamā	shyness often caused by being asked to do something in an inappropriate cultural context
whakamua	forward motion
whakapapa	genealogy, cultural identity, family tree
whakarongo mai	listen
whakataki	introduction
whakatika	make amends
whakawhanaungatanga	building relationships
whānau	literally means the extended family . . . in this context it is used to describe people working co-operatively and collaboratively for a particular purpose
whanaungatanga	relationships
wharekura	Māori immersion (language) secondary school

REFERENCES

Alberti, R., & Emmons, M. (1986). Your perfect right: A guide to assertive living. California: Impact Publishers.

Alderman, M. (1999). Motivation for achievement: Possibilities for teaching and learning. Mahwah, NJ: Lawrence Erlbaum Associates.

Ashman, A., & Elkins, J. (Eds.). (1998). Educating children with special needs (3rd ed.). Sydney: Prentice-Hall.

Barlow, C. (1993). Tikanga whakaaro: Key concepts in Māori culture. Auckland: Oxford University Press.

Bateman, S. (2003). Have a heart: Social relationships as the defining dimension in the learning classroom. Unpublished paper. Hamilton: Ministry of Education.

Beane, J. (1997). Curriculum integration: Designing the core of democratic education. New York: Teachers College Press.

Bennett, C. (1995). Comprehensive multicultural education; theory and practice (3rd ed.). Boston: Allyn & Brown.

Bevan-Brown, J. (1999). A cultural audit for teachers. Looking out for Māori learners with special needs. set special 1999: Special education, item 8.

Bevan-Brown, J. (2003). The cultural self-review: Providing culturally effective, inclusive education for Māori learners. Wellington: New Zealand Council for Educational Research.

Bishop, R. (1996). Addressing issues of self-determination and legitimation in kaupapa Māori research. In B. Webber (Ed.), He Paepae Korero, research perspectives in Māori education (pp. 143–160). Wellington: New Zealand Council for Educational Research.

Bishop, R., Berryman, M., Glynn, T., McKinley, E., Devine, N., & Richardson, C. (2002). The experiences of Māori children in the year 9 and year 10 classroom: Part 1 the scoping exercise. Paper presented to the Research Division of the Ministry of Education.

Bishop, R., Berryman, M., Richardson, C., & Tiakiwai, S. (2002). Te Kotahitanga: The experiences of year 9 and 10 Māori students in mainstream classrooms. Draft final report to the Ministry of Education. Report to the Ministry of Education, September 2002. Hamilton: University of Waikato.

Bishop, R., & Glynn, T. (1999). Culture counts: Changing power relations in education. Palmerston North: Dunmore Press.

Brown, D. (2002). Preparing for inclusive education through effective teaching. A thesis submitted in fulfilment of the requirements for the degree of Doctor of Philosophy. Hamilton: University of Waikato.

Brown, D., & Thomson, C. (2000). Cooperative learning in New Zealand schools. Palmerston North: Dunmore Press.

Brown, W., & Simons, R. (1997). Ethnic identity and attitudes toward school: Sources of variation in the educational achievement of African-American high school students. Delaware: University of Delaware, Department of Psychology.

Burgess, B. (1992). Referring at-risk students to activity centres. MEd thesis. Palmerston North: Massey University.

Canter, L., & Canter, M. (1992). Assertive discipline: Positive behaviour management for today's classroom. Santa Monica: Lee Canter & Associates.

Charles, C. (1999). Building classroom discipline (6th ed.). New York: Addison Wesley Longman.

Clark, E., Smith, L., & Pomare, M. (1996). Alternative education provisions. Discussion paper. Wellington: Te Puni Kokiri.

Clay, M. (1985). Engaging with the school system: A study of interactions in new entrant classrooms. New Zealand Journal of Educational Studies, 20 (1), 20–38.

Clay, M. (1993). An observation survey of early literacy achievement. Auckland: Heinemann.

Corson, D. (1993). Language, minority education, and gender: Linking social justice and power. Toronto: Ontario Institute for Studies in Education.

Coxon, E., Jenkins, K., Marshall, J., & Massey, L. (Eds.). (1994). The politics of learning and teaching in Aotearoa-New Zealand. Palmerston North: Dunmore Press.

Cross, T.L., Bazron, B.J., Dennis, K.W., & Isaacs, M.R. (1989). Towards a culturally competent system of care, Volume 1. Washington, DC: National Technical Assistance Centre for Children's Mental Health, Georgetown University Child Development Centre.

Cummings, C. (2000). Winning strategies for classroom management. Alexandria, Va: Association for Supervision and Curriculum Development.

Department of Education. (1973). Report of the committee on communication between schools and parents. Wellington: Department of Education.

Durie, M. (1994). Whaiora: Māori health development. Auckland: Oxford University Press.

Durie, M. (2001). A framework for considering Māori educational achievement. Paper presented to Ministry of Education staff. Wellington. 9 August 2001.

Education and Science Committee of the House of Representatives. (1995). Inquiry into children in education at risk through truancy and behavioural problems. Report of the Education and Science Committee, first session, forty fourth Parliament. Wellington: New Zealand Government.

Eisner, E. (1994). The educational imagination: On the design and evaluation of school programs (3rd ed.). New York: Macmillan.

Fergusson, D., Horwood, L., & Lloyd, M. (1991). Family ethnicity, social background and scholastic achievement: An eleven year longitudinal study. New Zealand Journal of Educational Studies, 26, (1), 49–63.

Ford, B., Obiakor, F., & Patton, J. (Eds.). (1995). Effective education of African-American exceptional learners: New perspectives. Austin: PROED.

Franklin, B. (Ed.). (1998). When children don't learn: Student failure and the culture of teaching. New York: Teachers College Press.

Fraser, D., Moltzen, R., & Ryba, K. (2000). Learners with special needs in Aotearoa/New Zealand (2nd ed.). Palmerston North: Dunmore Press.

Gadd, B. (1976). Cultural difference in the classroom: Special needs of Māori in Pakeha schools. Auckland: Heinemann Education.

Galloway, D. (1985). Schools, pupils and special educational needs. London: Croom Helm.

Garner, P., & Gains, C. (1996). Models of intervention for pupils with emotional and behavioural difficulties. British Journal of Learning Support, 11 (4), 141–145.

Gay, G. (2000). Culturally responsive teaching: Theory, research and practice. New York: Teachers College Press.

Gilmore, A., Croft, C., & Reid, N. (1981). Burt word reading test. Teachers manual. Wellington: New Zealand Council for Educational Research.

Giroux, H. (1994). Disturbing pleasures: Learning popular culture. New York: Routledge.

Glasser, W. (1993). The quality school teacher. New York: Harper Perennial.

Glynn, T. (1997). The Treaty in the context of education in Aotearoa. Seminar presented at Education Leadership Centre, University of Waikato, Hamilton.

Glynn, T. (1998). A collaborative approach to teacher development: New initiatives in special education. Paper presented to the 28th annual conference of the Australian Teacher Education Association, Melbourne, Australia.

Glynn, T., Berryman, M., Atvars, K., & Harawira, W. (1997). He Awhina Mātua. Final report to the Ministry of Education, Wellington.

Glynn, T., & Bishop, R. (1995). Cultural issues in educational research: A New Zealand perspective. He Pukenga Korero, 1 (1), 37–43.

Gollnick, D., & Chinn, P. (1994). Multicultural education in a pluralistic society. Columbus, OH: Merrill/Palmer Hall.

Good, T., & Brophy, J. (1994). Looking in classrooms. New York: Harper-Collins College Publications.

Grace, J. (1995). Tuwharetoa: A history of the Māori people of the Taupo district. Auckland: Reed.

Graham, J. (2003). Kanohi ki te kanohi: Establishing partnerships between schools and Māori communities. set: Research information for teachers. 2, 8–12.

Gudykunst, W. (1994). Bridging differences: Effective intergroup communication. Thousand Oaks, CA: Sage Publications.

Guerra, N., Attar, B., & Weissberg, R. (1997). Prevention of aggression and violence among inner-city youth. In D. Stoff, J. Breiling, & J. Maser (Eds.), Handbook of antisocial behaviour (pp. 375–383). New York: Wiley.

Hamilton, B. (1992). Cultural identity: Whakamana tangata. Wellington: Quest Rapuara.

Hardman, M., Drew, C., & Egan, M.W. (1999). Human exceptionality, society, school and family (6th ed.). Sydney: Allyn & Bacon.

Harker, R. (1978). Cognitive style, environment and school achievement: A cross-cultural study. Palmerston North: Education Department, Massey University.

Harker, R., & Nash, R. (1996). Academic outcomes and school effectiveness: Type "A" and type "B" effects. New Zealand Journal of Educational Studies, 31 (2), 143–170.

Harris, K.C. (1996). Collaboration within a multicultural society – issues for consideration. Rase: Remedial & Special Education, 17 (6), 355–362.

Henare, M. (1999). Sustainable social policy. In J. Boston, P. Dalziel, & S. St John (Eds.), Redesigning the welfare state in New Zealand: Problems, policies, prospects. (pp. 39–59). Oxford: University Press.

Henderson, A. (1987). The evidence continues to grow: Parent involvement improves school achievement. Columbia, MD: National Committee for Citizens in Education.

Hohepa, M. (1999). Hei tautoko i te reo: Māori language regeneration and whānau bookreading practices. Unpublished PhD thesis. University of Auckland.

Hotere, A. New Zealand Education Review. (1997). Suspension concerns. 16 September, p. 1.

Johnson, D., Johnson, R., & Maruyama, G. (1983). Interdependence and interpersonal attraction among heterogeneous and homogeneous individuals: A theoretical formulation and meta-analysis of the research. Review of Educational Research, 68, 446–452.

Jones, F. (1987). Positive classroom instruction. New York: McGraw-Hill.

Kallam, M., Hoernicke, P., & Coser, P. (1994). Native Americans and behavior disorders. In Peterson & Ishii-Jordan (Eds.), Multicultural issues in the education of students with behavioral disorders. Cambridge, Mass.: Brookline Books.

Kauffman, J. (1993). How we might achieve the radical reform of special education. Exceptional Children, 60 (1), 6–16.

Kauffman, J. (1997). Characteristics of emotional and behavioural disorders of children and youth (6th ed.). Upper Saddle River, NJ: Prentice-Hall Inc.

Kawagley, A., & Barnhardt, R. (1997). Education indigenous place: Western science meets native reality. Fairbanks: University of Alaska.

Kelly, K. (1990). Let someone else deal with them: A study of students referred to an activity centre. set: Research Information for Teachers, 1, item 4.

King, M. (Ed.). (1975). Te ao hurihuri: The world moves on: Aspects of Māoritanga. Wellington: Hicks Smith.

Kounin, J. (1977). Discipline and group management in classrooms (Rev. ed.). New York: Holt, Rinehart & Winston.

Ladson-Billings, G. (1990). Culturally relevant teaching: Effective instruction for black students. The College Board Review, 155, 20–25.

Ladson-Billings, G. (1994). What we can learn from multicultural education research. Education Leadership, May, 22–26.

Ladson-Billings, G. (1995). Toward a theory of culturally relevant pedagogy. American Educational Research Journal, 32 (3), 465–491.

Lipman, P. (1995). Bringing out the best in them: The contribution of culturally relevant teachers to educational reform. Theory into Practice, 34 (3), Summer.

Lose, J. (2000). Beverley lives for teaching. Sunday News, 12 November, p. 12. Auckland: Independent Newspapers Limited.

Macfarlane, A. (1995). Constructing values education programmes in a centre for special learners: A collective responsibility: Me whakaputaina te turanga, tena pea ka tika. Unpublished MSocSci dissertation, University of Waikato.

Macfarlane A. (2000a). Listening to culture: Māori principles and practices applied to classroom management. set: Research Information for Teachers, 2, 23–28.

Macfarlane, A. (2000b). The value of Māori ecologies in special education. In D. Fraser & R. Moltzen (Eds.), Learners with special needs in Aotearoa New Zealand (2nd ed). (pp. 77–98). Palmerston North: Dunmore Press.

Macfarlane, A. (2000). The value of Māori ecologies in the study of human development. In L. Bird & W. Drewery (Eds.), Part two: Māori perspectives on development (pp. 46–51). Auckland: McGraw-Hill.

Macfarlane, A. (2003). Culturally inclusive pedagogy for Māori students experiencing learning and behaviour difficulties. PhD thesis. University of Waikato.

Macfarlane, A.H. (1997). The Hikairo rationale teaching students with emotional and behavioural difficulties: A bicultural approach. Waikato Journal of Education, 3, 153–168.

Macfarlane, A.H. (2002). Restorying the individual: The cultural dimension of special education in three Te Arawa sites. Journal of Māori and Pacific Development, 3, 82–89.

Macfarlane, A., & Glynn, T. (2001). Cultural epistemology in a national special education curriculum in New Zealand. Kairanga, 2, 4–10.

Macfarlane, A., Glynn, T., Presland, I., & Greening, S. (2000). Māori culture and literacy learning: A bicultural approach. In L. Peer & G. Reid (Eds.),

Multilingualism, literacy and dyslexia: A challenge for educators, (pp. 120–128). London: David Fulton.

Macfarlane, J. (2003). Te Whare Tauira. A presentation prepared for developing partnerships between a school and its community. Hamilton: University of Waikato.

McElrea, F. (1994). The intent of the children and young persons' and their families act: Restorative justice. Youth Law Review, July–September, pp. 4–9. Auckland: Youth Law Project.

McElrea, F.W.M. (1996). Education, discipline and restorative justice. Butterworths Family Law Journal, December, 91–93.

McInerney, D., & McInerney, V. (1998). Educational psychology: Constructing learning (2nd ed.). Sydney: Prentice-Hall.

McKinley, S. (2002). Māori parents and education Ko Ngā Mātua Māori me te Mātauranga. Wellington: New Zealand Council for Educational Research.

McNamara, S., & Moreton, G. (1995). Changing behaviour: Teaching children with emotional and behavioural difficulties in primary and secondary classrooms. London: David Fulton.

McNaughton, S. (1995). Patterns of emergent literacy: Processes of development and transition. Auckland: Oxford University Press.

Marsden, M. (1975). God, man and universe: A Māori view. In M. King (Ed.), Te Ao Hurihuri, (pp. 117–137). Auckland: Reed.

Medcalf, J. (1995). Co-operative learning and peer tutoring strategies for inclusive education. Reading Forum NZ, 2, 11–19.

Metge, J. (1983). Learning and teaching: He tikanga Māori. Wellington: Department of Education.

Ministry of Education. (1993). The New Zealand curriculum framework: Te Anga Mātauranga o Aotearoa. Wellington: Ministry of Education.

Ministry of Education. (1996). The suspension statistics report. Hamilton: Ministry of Education Operations Office.

Ministry of Education. (1997a). Reading and beyond: Discovering language through Ready to Read. Wellington: Learning Media.

Ministry of Education. (1997b). School entry assessment/Aromatawai urunga-a-kura (SEA/AKA). Wellington: Learning Media.

Ministry of Education. (2002). Ngā Haeata Mātauranga: Annual report on Māori education 2000/2001 and direction for 2002. Wellington: Group Māori, Ministry of Education.

Mitchell, H.A., & Mitchell, M.J. (1988). Profile of Māori pupils with high marks in School Certificate English and mathematics. Volume 1: Report. A report prepared for the Department of Education, Wellington.

Morrisey, M. (1997). The uses of culture. Journal of Intercultural Studies, 18 (2), 93.

Ogbu, J. (1983). Minority status and schooling in plural societies. Comparative Education Review, 2 (2), 168–190.

Patterson, J. (1992). Exploring Māori values. Palmerston North: Dunmore Press.

Penetito, W. (1996). Te Mataora: An intervention strategy for the development of Māori teacher education. Paper presented at the annual conference of the New Zealand Association for Research in Education, Nelson, 5–8 December.

Penniman, T. (Ed.). (1986). Makereti: The old-time Māori. Auckland: New Women's Press.

Pere, R. (1994). Ako: Concepts and learning the Māori tradition. Wellington: Expo.

Petersen, R., & Ishii-Jordan, S. (Eds.). (1994). Multicultural issues in the education of students with behavioural disorders. Cambridge, Mass: Brookline Books.

Phinney, J., & Rotheram, M. (1987). Children's ethnic socialization: Pluralism and development. Newbury Park: Sage Publications.

Pierce, C. (1996). The importance of classroom climate for at-risk learners. In set special: Students at risk, item 10.

Pollard, D. (2002). Who will socialize African American students in contemporary public schools? African American Education, 2, 3–21.

Reynolds, M., & Birch, J. (1988). Adaptive mainstreaming a primer for teachers and principals. New York: Longman.

Ritchie, J. (1963). The making of a Māori. Wellington: Reed.

Ritchie, J. (1992). Becoming bicultural. Wellington: Huia Publishers.

Ritchie, J., & Ritchie, J. (1983). Polynesian child rearing: An alternative model. Alternative Lifestyles, 5 (3), 126–141.

Robinson, T., & Ginter, E. (1999). Introduction to the Journal of Counseling & Development's special issue on racism. Journal of Counseling & Development, 77 (1), Winter, 3.

Rogers, W. (1997). Behaviour management: A whole-school approach. Melbourne: Scholastic.

Rothbaum, F., Weisz, J., Pott, M., Miyake, K., & Morelli, G. (2000). Attachment and culture: Security in United States of America and Japan. American Psychologist, 55 (10), 1093–1104.

Ruru, G. (2001). A taste of success: Ngāti Whakaue Enrichment Unit – Ngongotahā School, Rotorua. Reading Forum Journal, July.

Rutter, M., Maugham, B., Mortimer, P., & Ouston, J. (1979). Fifteen thousand hours: Secondary schools and their effects on children. London: Open Books.

Salmond, A. (1975). Hui: A study of Māori ceremonial gatherings. Wellington: Reed Methuen.

Senge, P., Cambron-McCabe, N., Lucas, T., Smith, B., Dutton, J., & Kleiner, A. (2001). Schools that learn: A fifth discipline fieldbook for educators, parents, and everyone who cares about education. New York: Doubleday.

Sleeter, C., & Grant, C. (1999). Making choices for multicultural education: Five approaches to race, class, and gender. Upper Saddle River, NJ: Merrill.

Smith, C., & Laslett, R. (1993). Effective classroom management: A teacher's guide (2nd ed.). London: Routledge.

Smith, G. (1992). Education: Biculturalism or separatism. In Novitz, D., & Willmott, B. (Eds.), New Zealand in Crisis. (pp. 157–165). Wellington: Government Print.

Smith, G. (1995). Whakaoho whānau: New formations of whānau as an innovative intervention into Māori cultural and educational crises. He Pukenga Korero, 1 (1), 18–36.

Smith, L. (1992). Engaging in history: Kura Kaupapa Māori and the implications for curriculum. In G. McCulloch (Ed.), The school curriculum in New Zealand: History, theory, policy and practice (2nd ed.), (pp. 219–231). Palmerston North: Dunmore Press.

Smith, L. (1999). Decolonising methodologies: Research and indigenous peoples. Dunedin: University of Otago Press.

Smith, T., Polloway, E., Patton, J., & Dowdy, C. (2001). Teaching students with special needs in inclusive settings (2nd ed.). Needham Heights, MA: Allyn & Bacon.

Smith, T., Polloway, E., Patton, J., & Dowdy, C. (2001). Teaching students with special needs in inclusive settings (3rd ed.). Boston: Allyn & Bacon.

Stafford, D. (1967). Te Arawa: A history of the Arawa people. Wellington and Auckland: Reed.

Stainback, W., & Stainback, S. (1990). Support networks for inclusive schooling: Interdependent integrated education. Baltimore: P.H. Brooks.

Stanford, G. (1997). Successful urban African-American teachers. Pennyslvania: University of Delaware.

Steele, C. (1992). Race and the schooling of Black Americans. Atlantic Monthly, 269, 68–78.

Tate, H. (1990). The unseen world. New Zealand Geographic, 5, 87–92.

Te Puni Kokiri. (1998). Māori Education Commission Report 2. Report to the Ministry of Māori Affairs. Wellington: Author.

Vercoe, A. (1999). Resistance in Māori education: A critique of Kura Kaupapa Māori. Waikato Journal of Education, 1 (1), 119–135.

Walker, J., & Shea, T. (1999). Behaviour management: A practical approach for educators (7th ed.). New Jersey: Prentice Hall.

Walker, R. (1973). Biculturalism in education. In D. Bray & C. Hill (Eds.), Polynesian and Pakeha in New Zealand education (Vol. 1). (pp. 110–112). Auckland: Heinemann.

Walker, R. (1991). Liberating Māori from educational subjugation. Auckland: Research Unit for Māori Education, University of Auckland.

Wallace, G., Larsen, G., & Elksnin, L. (1992). Educational assessment of learning problems. Boston: Allyn & Bacon.

Williams, H. (1971). A dictionary of the Māori language (7th ed.). Wellington: Government Printer.

Winzer, M., & Mazurek, K. (1998). Special education in multicultural contexts. New Jersey: Prentice-Hall.

Wolfendale, S. (1992). Applying educational psychology: Locations and orientations. In S. Wolfendale, T. Bryans, M. Fox, A. Labram, & S. Sigston (Eds.), The profession and practice of educational psychology: Future directions, (pp. 1–16). London: Cassell Educational Limited.

Yibing, W. (2000). Learning and teaching on-line and virtualisation of education. A panel debate on critical issues at the sixth international conference of UNESCO – ACEID, Bangkok, Thailand, December.

Young-Loveridge, J.M. (1994). Supermarket maths game: A diagnostic tool for assessing early mathematics. Hamilton: University of Waikato.

The Cultural Self-Review:
Providing culturally effective, inclusive education
for Māori learners

Jill Bevan-Brown

The Cultural Self-Review provides a structure and process that teachers from early childhood centres through to secondary schools can use to explore how well they cater for Māori learners, including those with special needs. It is a user-friendly resource that enables strengths to be celebrated and built on, weaknesses to be identified and worked on, and communication between teachers, parents, whānau, and the Māori community to be promoted for the ultimate benefit of everyone concerned.

Central to the book is a cultural input framework which provides a set of principles for analysing programme components including: environment, personnel, policy, processes, content, resources, assessment, and administration. While there is an emphasis on practical ideas in this guide for conducting a cultural self-review, a recipe-book approach is not recommended. Schools and early childhood services will be able to use the ideas as a springboard for discussion and for developing strategies that meet their particular needs and which are appropriate for their unique circumstances.

NZCER 2003   ISBN 1-877293-25-3   RRP: $27.00

ORDER FROM

NZCER Sales, PO Box 3237, Wellington

Phone: 04 802 1450   Fax: 04 384 7933

Email: sales@nzcer.org.nz

A full list of NZCER publications is available on the Internet.

Check out our site at www.nzcer.org.nz

Māori Parents and Education
Ko Ngā Mātua Māori me te Mātauranga

Sheridan McKinley with Anne Else

This book presents the perspectives of Māori parents as they talk about education and their aspirations for, and their concerns about, their children's schooling. It provides valuable insights which may contribute to shaping better home-school relationships for Māori parents and children.

The parents in the study wanted their children to have a better education than they had, and expressed a strong wish to be involved in their child's schooling. The key factor is school outreach. When teachers reach out into the community, showing their respect for the relationships and activities which matter for Māori parents and their children, partnership with parents appears to be more readily achieved. How well Māori children do at school is strongly linked with how well parents and children relate to school staff.

This book is an abridged version of the major research report Māori Parents and Education: Ko Ngā Mātua Māori me te Mātauranga.

NZCER 2002   ISBN 1-877293-13-X   RRP: $19.80

ORDER FROM

NZCER Sales, PO Box 3237, Wellington
Phone: 04 802 1450   Fax: 04 384 7933
Email: sales@nzcer.org.nz

A full list of NZCER publications is available on the Internet.
Check out our site at www.nzcer.org.nz

www.ingramcontent.com/pod-product-compliance
Lightning Source LLC
Chambersburg PA
CBHW080555270326
41929CB00019B/3324